AUSTIN
Like a Local

BY THE PEOPLE WHO CALL IT HOME

AUSTIN
Like a Local

BY THE PEOPLE WHO CALL IT HOME

Contents

EAT

DRINK

SHOP

ARTS & CULTURE

NIGHTLIFE

OUTDOORS

meet the locals

NICOLAI MCCRARY

Nicolai landed in Austin in 2008 and has called the city home ever since. When he's not pursuing his career in food photography, he can usually be found on one of Austin's many bike trails, trying out the latest taco trucks, or hosting Malaysian pop-up dinners around town.

JESSICA DEVENYNS

As they say, although she wasn't born in Texas, she got there as fast as she could. Jessi enjoys hiking through the beautiful Hill Country greenbelts, languishing away afternoons on patios with a coffee in hand, and learning to grow green things on urban farms.

JUSTINE HARRINGTON

Travel writer Justine moved to Austin to be with her people: rescue dog-loving outdoor enthusiasts and live music fans. She enjoys volunteering with Austin Mutual Aid and rallying for progressive causes. In her downtime, you'll probably find her browsing the city's indie bookshops.

Austin

WELCOME TO THE CITY

Cattle wranglers, football players, two-stepping old-timers: forget those time-worn images of Texas. This is Austin, a city that's as politically liberal and socially diverse as Texas is big. So what makes an Austinite? A love of tacos. Just kidding (well, kinda, this city is Tex-Mex obsessed). Austinites are laid-back, warm-hearted, and community spirited. This is a place where everyone is greeted with a "Hey y'all"; where the hippies who moved here in the 70s and techies who followed their companies to the Silicon Hills share a coffee shop; and where born-and-bred Texans and generations of immigrants spearhead campaigns to support their local theater or bookstore.

And, boy, have Austinites had to band together over the years. Flash floods, winter storms, and decades of segregation have all left their mark on the cityscape. Glinting skyscrapers overlook historic bungalows, and swanky cocktail bars sit kitty-corner to no-frills food trucks. And though rising rents have pushed out some of the music venues and honky-tonks that earned this city the title of "Live Music Capital of the World," Austin still moves to a unique beat.

"Keep Austin weird," locals cry. And beneath the facade of strip malls, chain restaurants, and big tech companies, Austin's quirky soul is alive and kicking in indie boutiques, offbeat graffiti, and downright wacky attractions. And that's exactly where this book will take you. We know the places that Austinites adore, from the BBQ joints they'll camp outside for to the swimming spots they'll linger in till late. Of course, these pages can't capture every local's experience but rather offer a snapshot of the city.

Whether you're a long-time local looking to shake up your routine or a visitor seeking inspiration for your first trip, this book will help you discover the real spirit of the city. So buckle up, and enjoy Austin the local way.

Liked by the locals

"Austin is the biggest small town that you'll ever live in. I love the contrast of knowing the name of my neighborhood barista but also being able to see world-class music acts and art shows. I couldn't ask for more."

JESSICA DEVENYNS, WRITER

Escaping the heat is a common theme throughout the year, but Austin still has distinct seasons, each with their own traditions and events.

Austin
THROUGH THE YEAR

SPRING

FESTIVAL FUN
Despite a short winter, locals are still grateful for the arrival of spring. And in the Live Music Capital of the World, there's only one way to celebrate: at an outdoor music festival like SXSW or Pachanga Presents.

BLOSSOMING BLUEBONNETS
In March and April, the city comes to a halt – literally – as locals stop to admire deep-blue carpets of bluebonnets, the state flower, in their neighbors' gardens and on roadsides.

FARMERS' MARKETS
Each weekend, Austinites head to their nearest pop-up market to pick up farm-fresh produce, chow down on tacos from top-notch trucks, and enjoy live entertainment.

SUMMER

SUMMER SWIMS
Carrying coolers and inflatable tubes, locals seek relief from the sweltering temperatures at the city's swimming holes and outdoor pools.

OUTDOOR MOVIE THEATERS
As evenings become longer and warmer, screens pop up across Austin. Classic movies are enjoyed with picnic blankets, deck chairs, and ice-cold beers. The coolest screenings? Deep Eddy's Splash Party Movie Nights, held in Texas's oldest swimming pool.

THE GREAT ESCAPE

At the height of summer, Austin reaches melting point and locals flee the city in search of colder climes. They migrate to the Hill Country for walks and wine tastings, or relive their summer camp days with sleep outs in state parks.

FALL

PATIO PARTIES

After chasing air-conditioning for months, Austinites finally return to their beloved alfresco lifestyle with fall's easing temperatures. People (and their pooches) park up on patios for coffee, cocktails, and everything in between.

COMMUNITY CELEBRATIONS

Austinites are proud of their diverse city and celebrate its many communities. In fall, the LGBTQ+ community and its allies come together for Pride, while Latin American culture is celebrated on Mexican Independence Day and during Hispanic Heritage Month.

HARVEST TIME

Fall marks the start of the wine harvest season, and budding sommeliers flock to dedicated festivals and vineyards

to sample the new vintages. Beer fans aren't forgotten, with breweries releasing seasonal brews, including pumpkin craft beers. Nothing says fall like a bit of spiced pumpkin, after all.

WINTER

HOLIDAY CHEER

Come December, the holidays get a uniquely Austin spin. Tacos are stuffed with turkey, musicians play Christmas tracks on repeat, and weird and wacky lights festoon 37th Street, including the likes of life-size, illuminated dinosaurs and fairy lights spelling out "Joy to the Weird."

POLAR PLUNGE

Whether winter brings mild or freezing temperatures, Austinites ring in the new year with a refreshing dip in a swimming hole on New Year's Day. Barton Springs hosts the biggest splash, with hordes of goose-pimpled revelers jumping in here.

FREE WEEK

Austinites know how to beat the postholiday blues – music. And during the first week of January, venues open their doors for music fans to enjoy hundreds of local music acts for free.

There's an art to being an Austinite, from the do's and don'ts of eating out to negotiating the city's streets. Here's a breakdown of all you need to know.

Austin
KNOW-HOW

For a directory of health and safety resources, safe spaces, and accessibility information, turn to page 186. For everything else, read on.

EAT
As you may have heard, Austin is a food truck haven, and locals chow down on Tex-Mex, BBQ, and other street food at all hours of the day and night. There are no real hard-and-fast rules when it comes to mealtimes, or when to eat what. Tacos for breakfast? It's an Austin institution.

At upscale restaurants, reservations are a must. But there's never a need to dress up – unless you want to, of course.

DRINK
Austin's patio culture is legendary, and nearly every bar and café has a cute outdoor spot. Locals are notoriously fond of day drinking, with people chatting over frozen margaritas and glasses of Texan rosé at any time of the day. Those who hold out till 4pm are generally rewarded with happy hour deals.

That's not to say that it's all about boozing. The coffee revolution has reached this corner of Texas, with cold brews replacing standard drip coffees. And this health-conscious city takes juices and smoothies very seriously.

SHOP
The phrase "keep Austin weird" is more than just a marketing slogan – it's a way of life. Austinites prefer to shop at indie stores, farmers' markets, and local boutiques over chain stores.

Most shops open around 10am, and close at 6pm. Sales associates are generally helpful and friendly, so don't be surprised if they start doling out advice and coaxing you toward a fitting room. Oh, and although they're not outlawed, plastic bags are universally frowned upon, so carry a tote.

ARTS & CULTURE
Austin's big museums and galleries aren't cheap to enter, with some costing upward of $10. Fortunately, many have free admission days. Theater tickets are similarly pricey, but you can find deals online. The dress code is the same throughout Austin: jeans all the way.

NIGHTLIFE
Music is the lifeblood of the city and dominates the nighttime scene. Nights out often start in the late afternoon with country music at a honky-tonk or with a happy hour deal at a dive bar. After, locals push on to a live music venue or club. Austinites don't pull all-nighters, especially as most clubs close by 2am. Wherever you go, expect a low-key dress code and to have to show ID.

OUTDOORS
Austinites are an outdoorsy bunch. On sunny days, they flock to the city's parks, greenbelts, and swimming holes to escape the heat. Picnicking is permitted in the city's green spaces, but alcohol typically isn't. Be sure to pick up your trash – littering carries a hefty fine (and dirty looks from eco-conscious locals). Austin has a growing homeless population, so it's not unheard of to be approached for food in the city's parks.

Keep in mind

Here are some tips and tidbits that will help you fit in like a local.

» **Keep cash handy** Much of the city is cashless, but a select few places remain cash only. So it's probably best to carry both cards and dollars.

» **No smoking** Lighting up is a definite no-no in public places, including parks, restaurants, and bars. If you have to smoke, do so in a designated spot outside.

» **Always tip** Adding at least 15, if not 20, percent to your bill is a must at restaurants, bars, and even food trucks.

» **Stay protected** Wear a strong sunblock and carry a water bottle with you at all times. This city is hot.

GETTING AROUND

Austin is a pretty small city – it measures just 7 miles by 7 miles – and though it's built up of neighborhoods, some only comprise a handful of blocks. Generally speaking, though, locals think of Austin both physically and culturally as five distinct areas – north, south, east, west, and Downtown. Lady Bird Lake (or Town Lake, as it's called by locals) divides the north and south parts of the city, while Congress Avenue is the dividing line for addresses east and west. Bordered by Lamar Boulevard to the west and I-35 to the east, Downtown – the cultural center of the city – straddles both east and west. Austin is organized in not one but seven grid systems, meaning that some roads jut out at odd angles and streets that you would expect to be parallel, like West 28th and West 29th, are anything but. This can make navigation a little bit tricky at times.

To keep things simple, we've provided what3words addresses for each sight in this book, meaning you can quickly pinpoint exactly where you're heading.

On foot

The car is king when it comes to Austin's roads, but some neighborhoods, like Downtown, The Drag, and Rainey, are wonderfully walkable. That being said, walking in the midday heat is not recommended. Stick to the sidewalks as much as possible, and if you do need to stop and check a what3words location, step to the side, out of the way.

On wheels

Biking is not for the faint of heart here in car-happy Austin. If you're willing to brave it, avoid bigger roads like South Lamar altogether, wear a helmet, always signal when turning, and never listen to music while you ride.

The city's official bikeshare program, MetroBike, rents out bikes for one ride (for the bizarrely precise amount of $1.09 plus 23¢ per minute) or for 24 hours ($12.99). You can rent a MetroBike via the CapMetro and BCycle apps. Keep in mind that regardless of your pass or membership level, all MetroBikes must be returned to a docking station after 60 minutes. Yes, even if you've booked your bike for the whole day, you'll need to dock it every hour. Once you've docked your bike, you can check it back out for an additional hour using the app.
www.austin.bcycle.com

By public transportation

The Capital Metro Bus System covers the city, with 82 routes and 1,600 bus stops. But don't be alarmed – it's easy to use. Buy a ticket via the CapMetro app before boarding or ask the driver for a Single Ride or Day Pass – just remember that you will need exact change. When you want to board, motion to the driver; then, when you're about a block from your destination, trigger the stop signal by pushing the button or pulling the cord.

By car or taxi

Like the rest of Texas, Austin is car-centric. So using a rideshare app or rental car is the way to go if you're planning on zipping around to different parts of the city in a short period of time. Some of the most popular rideshare apps include Uber, Lyft, and the nonprofit RideAustin. Taxis are less common than rideshares, but if that's more your style Lone Star Cab Austin and Yellow Cab Austin are good options.

When driving, avoid getting on I-35, the Interstate Highway that bisects the city to the east of Congress Avenue, at rush hour (or anytime, really) if you can help it – the traffic is real. Be aware that Downtown is full of confusing one-way streets and parking is scarce, so be prepared to fork out some cash to park in a garage if necessary.
www.rideaustin.com

Download these

We recommend you download these apps to help you get about the city.

WHAT3WORDS
Your geocoding friend
A what3words address is a simple way to communicate any precise location on earth, using just three words. ///without.inserted.forecast, for example, is the code for the *Greetings From Austin* mural. Simply download the free what3words app, type a what3words address into the search bar, and you'll know exactly where to go.

CAPMETRO
Your local transportation service
With live departures, route maps, and an itinerary builder, the CapMetro app lays out all your best options for moving around the city. You can also buy tickets on the go through the app.

Austin is a patchwork of old and new neighborhoods, each with its own character and community. Here we take a look at some of our favorites.

Austin
NEIGHBORHOODS

12th Street Cultural District

After the 1928 Austin city plan forced Black Americans to relocate to the east side of the city, 12th Street became a hub for Black-owned businesses. Today, it remains so, with food trucks and boutiques keeping the place buzzing. *{map 2}*

Barton Hills

When outdoorsy Austinites want to escape the city, they head to leafy Barton Hills, an area known for its hiking trails, swimming spots, and scenic views. *{map 6}*

Central East Austin

You'd be hard-pressed to find an area with a better food scene than Central East's. Top-notch BBQ spots, taco trucks, and Italian bistros can all be found here. *{map 2}*

Cherrywood

Families love this quiet enclave of East Austin where coffee shops and taco truck owners know every local's order. *{map 3}*

Clarksville

Founded by freedman Charles Clark, this historic area was deprived of many basic utilities under the 1928 Austin city plan, until the 70s. Today, Clarksville attracts an arty crowd who hang out in the trendy local restaurants and wander around the area's many outdoor galleries. *{map 4}*

Crestview

This northern corner may still cling to its slightly seedy history (spot the strip clubs), but its collection of cool bars and breweries tempts young professionals to make this 'hood their home. *{map 6}*

Downtown

During the day, Austin's central business district is busy with techies putting in the hours. Come nightfall, the area's bars open their doors and office workers let loose on raucous 6th Street. *{map 1}*

The Drag

UT's local area is ruled by students staking out the coffee shops, browsing bookstores, and exploring the city's museums. On the weekend, families descend on these institutions for a cultural day out. {map 4}

East Cesar Chavez

Historically Mexican and Latin American, East Cesar Chavez is a colorful commotion of murals and independent boutiques. Unsurprisingly, you'll find some of the city's best Tex-Mex joints here, too. {map 2}

Hyde Park

Home to high-earning families, gorgeous Victorian houses, and popular juice bars and bakeries, Hyde Park is Austin at its most charming. {map 4}

Mueller

The city's old airport once occupied this site (hence the arrow-straight boulevards). After it closed in the 90s, the area was redeveloped as a sustainable residential community. These days, it's not the roar of jet engines you'll hear but the sounds of families relaxing in Mueller's modern parks

and eco-conscious friends stocking up on veggies at the farmers' markets. {map 3}

North Loop

Locals here (namely students and artists) will tell you North Loop is where Austin really stays weird. By and large the area's stores and homes have resisted the tide of gentrification. Expect anarchist bookstores, quirky bakeries, and eclectically decorated front yards. {map 4}

Rainey

Bars, bars, and more bars. Rainey's all about the good times, with neighborhood watering holes packed with young guns drinking under the fairy lights and listening to live music. {map 1}

Red River Cultural District

Want to know why Austin's called the "Live Music Capital of the World"? Head to Red River. Here, historic country music spots vie for space with heavy metal venues. The area's popular nightclubs keep the good vibes going late, too. {map 1}

South Congress

South Congress – or SoCo as locals call it – was once the center of the counter-culture that defined what keeps Austin weird. While swanky shops and boutique hotels have set up shop here, community bookstores and food trucks still serve the loyal locals. {map 5}

South First

Vintage clothes stores, third-wave coffeehouses, vibrant street art: SoCo's little sister is the epitome of laid-back cool, and Austin's hipsters love it. {map 5}

St. Elmo

Art studios, distilleries, and coffee roasteries have taken over St. Elmo's industrial complexes and made this nonresidential patch a weekend hub for fun-loving locals. {map 6}

Tarrytown

Hard to beat for that small-town feel, Tarrytown is known for its enviable (read: pricey) properties, bougie waterside cafés, and close-knit community. {map 6}

Austin
ON THE MAP

Whether you're looking for your new favorite spot or want to check out what each part of Austin has to offer, our maps – along with handy map references throughout the book – have you covered.

Colorado Ri

BEE CAVES ROA

BARTON
CREEK

TX-71

OAK HILL

US-290

SOUTH MOPAC EXPRES

DRIPPING
SPRINGS   US-290

BELTERRA

0 kilometers   5

0 miles   5

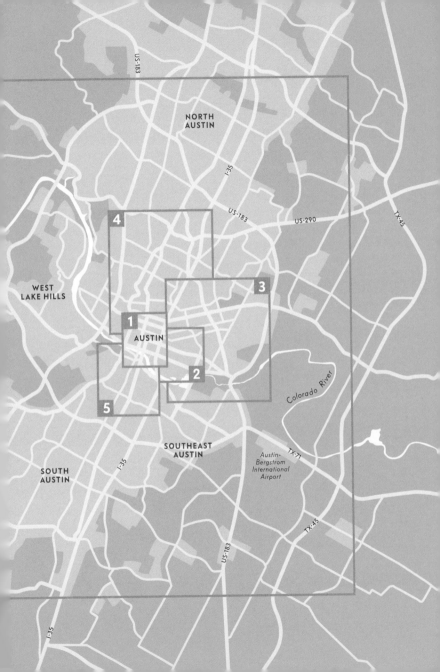

Pease
District Park

ENFIELD ROAD

JUDGE'S HILL

WEST 18TH STREET

Shoal Creek

CLARKSVILLE

WEST 15TH STREET

BLANCO STREET

S Good Company

WEST AVENUE

NUECES STREET

WEST 12TH STREET

STREET

STREET

Texas State Capitol

WEST 11TH STREET

Wally
Workman
Gallery
A

NORTH LAMAR BOULEVARD

WEST 9TH STREET

Texas African American
History Memorial **A**

EAST 11TH

E Swedish Hill

GUADALUPE

LAVACA

COLORADO ST

CONGRESS AVE

SAN JACINTO BLVD

S BookPeople

E Better Half
Coffee & Cocktails

WEST 6TH STREET

Whole
Foods **S**

WEST 5TH STREET

N Rio

Fallout Theater

N

Paramount
Theatre **A**

Here Nor There **D**

SEAHOLM

The Iron Bear
Roosevelt
Room

SFC Farmers'
Market Downtown **S**

D

The Hideout
Theatre **N**

Garage **D**

Midnight
Cowboy **D**

Museu
the We

Lora Reynolds Gallery **A**

D Comedor
E

N Summit

Highland Lounge **N**

Mexic-Arte
Museum **A**

Esther's
Follie

Austin Central
Library **A**

Ballet Austin **O**

Rain on 4th **N** **N**
Coconut Club **N**

Oilcan
Harry's **N**

Antone's **N**

Violet Crown
Cinema **A**

N

EAST 4TH STRE

DOWNTOWN

The Moody
Theater

SOUTH LAMAR BOULEVARD

WEST RIVERSIDE DRIVE

Colorado River

D Revolución
Coffee + Juice

Tau Ceti **A**

EAST CESAR CHAVEZ STREET

*Butler
Metro Park*

BARTON SPRINGS ROAD

SOUTH 1ST STREET

SOUTH CONGRESS AVE

RAINEY

RAINEY

RAINEY

Banger's

Half Step **D** **D**

Emma S. Barrientos Mexican
American Cultural Center **A**

0 meters   500
0 yards   500

MAP 1

E EAT

Better Half Coffee & Cocktails
(p40)

Comedor (p52)

Swedish Hill (p37)

D DRINK

Banger's (p74)

Garage (p79)

Half Step (p79)

Here Nor There (p76)

Midnight Cowboy (p77)

Revolución Coffee + Juice (p64)

Roosevelt Room (p76)

S SHOP

BookPeople (p100)

Good Company (p93)

SFC Farmers' Market
Downtown (p99)

Whole Foods (p96)

A ARTS & CULTURE

Austin Central Library (p114)

Emma S. Barrientos Mexican
American Cultural Center (p114)

Lora Reynolds Gallery (p123)

Mexic-Arte Museum (p123)

Museum of the Weird (p125)

Paramount Theatre (p118)

Tau Ceti (p130)

Texas African American History
Memorial (p113)

Violet Crown Cinema (p118)

Wally Workman Gallery (p120)

N NIGHTLIFE

Antone's (p144)

Barbarella (p140)

Cheer Up Charlies (p153)

Coconut Club (p142)

Elysium (p143)

Esther's Follies (p151)

Fallout Theater (p149)

The Hideout Theatre (p150)

Highland Lounge (p152)

The Iron Bear (p155)

Mohawk (p147)

The Moody Theater (p145)

Oilcan Harry's (p153)

Rain on 4th (p152)

Rio (p142)

Stubb's BBQ (p144)

Summit (p141)

The Velveeta Room (p148)

O OUTDOORS

Ballet Austin (p170)

EAST 15TH STREET

I-35

NORTH INTERSTATE 35

NAVASOTA STREET

Oakwood Cemetery

COMAL STREET

CHESTNUT AVENUE

12TH STREET CULTURAL DISTRICT

Ⓐ We Rise

Ⓔ Cuantos Tacos

EAST 12TH STREET

CHICON STREET

FOSTER HEIGHTS

RED RIVER STREET

Waller Creek

I-35

Ⓔ Franklin Barbecue

Ⓐ Texas Music Museum

Ⓔ J. Leonardi's Barbecue **Ⓢ Ⓔ** Apartment F

Ⓓ Nickel City

Ⓔ Hillside Farmacy **Ⓔ Ⓢ**

Ⓐ Tony's Jamaican Food

Ⓐ George Washington Carver Museum

ROSEWOOD AVENUE

Ⓢ Helm Boots **Ⓔ** Discada

Miranda Bennett Studio

Micklethwait Craft Meats

Ⓓ Figure 8 Coffee Purveyors

EAST 11TH STREET

CENTRAL EAST AUSTIN

Texas State Cemetery

Ⓞ Waller Creek Greenbelt Trail

EAST 7TH STREET

CHICON STREET

EAST AUSTIN

Ⓝ Violet Crown Social Club

Ⓔ Granny's Tacos **Ⓔ** Easy Tiger

The Volstead Lounge **Ⓝ Ⓓ** LoLo

Ⓝ White Horse

Ⓓ Blenders & Bowls

Ⓢ Salt & Time

Kitty Cohe **Ⓓ**

Tamale House East

Ⓔ Vixen's Wedding

Ⓓ Cuvée Coffee

Ⓓ APT 115

Ⓔ Joe's B

EAST 4TH STREET

EAST 5TH STREET

WALLER STREET

Ⓐ Women & Their Work

EAST CESAR CHAVEZ STREET

Greater Goods

EAST CESAR CHAVEZ

COMAL STREET

Mr. Natural **Ⓓ**

ROBERT T MARTINEZ JUNIOR STREET

HOLLY

Ⓞ E Te

Ⓐ grayDUCK Gallery

HOLLY STREET

CHICON STREET

PEDERNALES STREET

I-35

Ⓔ Launderette

0 meters 500
0 yards 500

Ⓞ Thursday Night Social Ride

Ⓞ Stand-Up Paddleboarding

Colorado R

MAP 2

Nixta

Doggy Creek

2

PLEASANT VALLEY ROAD

EAST 7TH STREET

PLEASANT VALLEY ROAD

Kemuri
Tatsu-ya

🅔 EAT

Cuantos Tacos *(p50)*

Discada *(p48)*

Easy Tiger *(p38)*

Franklin Barbecue *(p44)*

Granny's Tacos *(p34)*

Hillside Farmacy *(p34)*

J. Leonardi's Barbecue *(p47)*

Joe's Bakery *(p33)*

Kemuri Tatsu-ya *(p55)*

Launderette *(p35)*

Micklethwait Craft Meats *(p45)*

Nixta *(p43)*

Tamale House East *(p33)*

Tony's Jamaican Food *(p44)*

Vixen's Wedding *(p55)*

🅓 DRINK

APT 115 *(p83)*

Blenders & Bowls *(p65)*

Cuvée Coffee *(p63)*

Figure 8 Coffee
Purveyors *(p60)*

Greater Goods *(p61)*

Kitty Cohen's *(p79)*

LoLo *(p80)*

Mr. Natural *(p64)*

Nickel City *(p68)*

🅢 SHOP

Apartment F *(p107)*

Helm Boots *(p93)*

Miranda Bennett
Studio *(p95)*

Salt & Time *(p97)*

🅐 ARTS & CULTURE

George Washington Carver
Museum *(p126)*

grayDUCK Gallery *(p120)*

Texas Music Museum *(p112)*

We Rise *(p128)*

Women & Their Work *(p121)*

🅝 NIGHTLIFE

Violet Crown Social Club *(p155)*

The Volstead Lounge *(p140)*

White Horse *(p137)*

🅞 OUTDOORS

Esquina Tango *(p170)*

Stand-Up Paddleboarding *(p168)*

Thursday Night Social Ride *(p169)*

Waller Creek Greenbelt Trail *(p165)*

0 kilometers 1
0 miles 1

S Texas Farmers' Market

The Thinkery A N Austin Poetry Slam

MUELLER

O Mueller Lake Park

Cherrywood Coffeehouse D E El Mana

EAST 38½ ST

CHERRYWOOD

D La Fruta Feliz

MANOR RD

Butterfly Bar at the Vortex N D Bird Bird Biscuit

MANOR ROAD

EAST MARTIN LUTHER KING JR BOULEVARD

MLK

Sour Duck Market E A You're My Butter Half

CHESTNUT

Sahara Lounge N

EAST MLK

E Comadre Panadería EAST 12TH STREET

OAK SPRINGS DRIVE

CENTRAL EAST AUSTIN

ROSEWOOD AVENUE

EAST AUSTIN

The Paper + Craft Pantry S

Blackfeather Vintage Works S

Desnudo D Coffee

Boggy Creek Farm S

Ground Floor Theatre A

EAST 7TH STREET

East Austin Succulents S

Keith Kreeger Studios S

Southern Walnut Creek Trail O

EAST CESAR CHAVEZ

EAST 5TH STREET

GOVALLE

Drinks Lounge D EAST CESAR CHAVEZ STREET

Kinda Tropical D

JOHNSTON TERRACE

E Justine's

Colorado River

PLEASANT VALLEY ROAD

E Rosita's Al Pastor

Roy G. Guerrero Park

MAP 3

NGDALE ROAD

3

E EAT

Bird Bird Biscuit *(p32)*
Comadre Panadería *(p39)*
El Mana *(p48)*
Justine's *(p55)*
Rosita's Al Pastor *(p49)*
Sour Duck Market *(p36)*

D DRINK

Cherrywood Coffeehouse *(p63)*
Desnudo Coffee *(p61)*
Drinks Lounge *(p70)*
La Fruta Feliz *(p65)*
Kinda Tropical *(p70)*

S SHOP

Blackfeather Vintage Works *(p89)*
Boggy Creek Farm *(p98)*
East Austin Succulents *(p104)*
Keith Kreeger Studios *(p106)*
The Paper + Craft Pantry *(p105)*
Texas Farmers' Market *(p97)*

A ARTS & CULTURE

Ground Floor Theatre *(p117)*
The Thinkery *(p125)*
You're My Butter Half *(p129)*

N NIGHTLIFE

Austin Poetry Slam *(p148)*
Butterfly Bar at the Vortex *(p155)*
Sahara Lounge *(p141)*

O OUTDOORS

Mueller Lake Park *(p172)*
Southern Walnut Creek Trail *(p164)*

BERGSTROM EXPRESSWAY

Bolm
District
Park

olorado River

0 kilometers ———————————— 1
0 miles ———————————— 1

Ⓢ **Austin Pets Alive! Thrift**

Ⓔ **Paprika**

WEST KOENIG LANE

Ⓢ **Atown**

Ⓝ **Little Longhorn Saloon**

BRENTWOOD

Ⓔ **Fonda San Miguel**

BURNET ROAD

NORTH LAMAR BOULEVARD

Waller Creek

Ⓢ **BookWoman**

Ⓓ **Pinthouse Pizza**

WEST 45TH STREET

Ⓢ **Monkeywrench Books**

Ⓔ **Big Bertha's Paradise Vir**

Ⓓ **Epoch Coffee** Ⓢ Ⓢ Ⓢ **NORT LOO**

Shoal Creek

Room Service Vintage

Ⓢ **Zucchini Kill Bakery**

NORTH MOPAC EXPRESSWAY

OAKMONT HEIGHTS

WEST 35TH STREET

Ⓢ **South Congress Books**

Ⓓ **Draught House Pub & Brewery**

Ⓓ **People's Pharmacy**

Ⓓ Ⓢ **Blue Elephant**

Ⓐ **Hyde Park Theatre**

HYDE PARK

Ⓢ **First Light Book Shop**

ColdTowne Thea

EAST 45TH STREET

Ⓔ **Quack's** Ⓔ Ⓢ **Antonelli's Cheese Shop**

Ⓞ **Taiji & Qigong Meditation Center**

Ⓢ **Consuela Austin**

GUADALUPE STREET

EAST 38TH STREET

Ⓞ **Shoal Creek Trail**

Ⓔ **Musashino**

NORTH LAMAR BLVD

Ⓢ **Buffalo Exchange**

Ⓢ **Wheatsville Co-op**

OLD WEST AUSTIN

Waller Creek

RED RIVER STREET

CENTRAL AUSTIN

I-35

Ⓓ **Crown & Anchor Pub**

Ⓓ **The Hole in the Wall**

Ⓐ **Neill-Cochran House Museum**

Ⓐ **University of Texas Tower**

Bass Concert Hall

Ⓔ **Aster's Ethiopian Restaurant**

Ⓐ Ⓐ **LBJ Presidential Library**

Ⓐ **Hi, How Are You** Ⓐ Ⓐ **Harry Ransom Center** Ⓐ **The Color Inside**

ENFIELD ROAD

University of Texas

MANOR ROAD

Ⓝ **Josephine House**

THE DRAG

Ⓔ **Olamaie**

Ⓐ **Blanton Museum of Art**

LAVACA STREET

Ⓐ **Bullock State History Museum**

EAST MARTIN LUTHER KING JR

CLARKSVILLE

WEST END

EAST AUSTI

Ⓝ **Donn's Depot**

MAP 4

4

Ⓐ AFS
Cinema

ooken and Heard

arfly's

I-35

Mueller
Lake Park

AIRPORT BOULEVARD

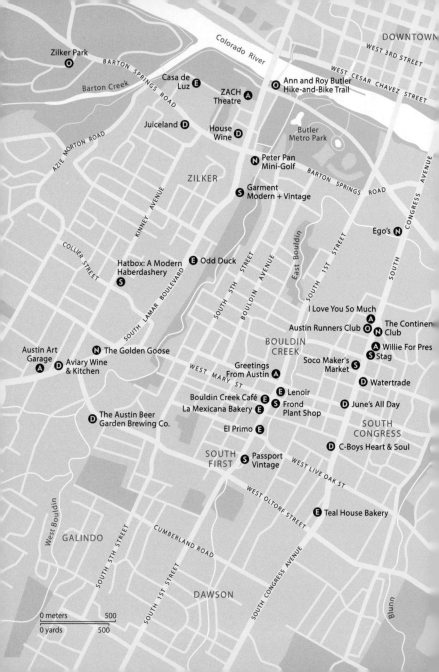

Zilker Park **O**

BARTON SPRINGS ROAD

Barton Creek

Casa de Luz **E**

ZACH Theatre **A**

AZIE MORTON ROAD

Juiceland **D**

House Wine **D**

Colorado River

WEST 3rd STREET

DOWNTOWN

WEST CESAR CHAVEZ STREET

Ann and Roy Butler Hike-and-Bike Trail **O**

Butler Metro Park

Peter Pan Mini-Golf **N**

ZILKER

Garment Modern + Vintage **S**

BARTON SPRINGS ROAD

SOUTH CONGRESS AVENUE

Ego's **N**

COLLIER STREET

Hatbox: A Modern Haberdashery **S**

Odd Duck **E**

KINNEY AVENUE

SOUTH 5TH STREET

BOULDIN AVENUE

East Bouldin

SOUTH 1ST STREET

SOUTH CONGRESS

SOUTH LAMAR BOULEVARD

I Love You So Much **A**

Austin Runners Club **O**

The Continental Club **N**

Austin Art Garage **A**

The Golden Goose **N**

Aviary Wine & Kitchen **D**

WEST MARY ST

Greetings From Austin **A**

BOULDIN CREEK

Soco Maker's Market **S**

Willie For Pres **A**

Stag **S**

Watertrade **D**

Bouldin Creek Café **E**

Lenoir **E**

La Mexicana Bakery **E**

Frond Plant Shop **S**

June's All Day **D**

The Austin Beer Garden Brewing Co. **D**

El Primo **E**

C-Boys Heart & Soul **D**

SOUTH FIRST

Passport Vintage **S**

WEST LIVE OAK ST

WEST OLTORF STREET

Teal House Bakery **E**

West Bouldin

GALINDO

SOUTH 5TH STREET

CUMBERLAND ROAD

SOUTH 1ST STREET

DAWSON

SOUTH CONGRESS AVENUE

Bluun

0 meters 500
0 yards 500

MAP 5

EAT

Bouldin Creek Café *(p41)*
Casa de Luz *(p43)*
El Primo *(p32)*
Lenoir *(p42)*
La Mexicana Bakery *(p38)*
Odd Duck *(p52)*
Teal House Bakery *(p36)*

DRINK

The Austin Beer Garden
   Brewing Co. *(p75)*
Aviary Wine & Kitchen *(p81)*
C-Boys Heart & Soul *(p70)*
House Wine *(p80)*
Juiceland *(p66)*
June's All Day *(p83)*
Watertrade *(p77)*

SHOP

Frond Plant Shop *(p106)*
Garment Modern + Vintage *(p91)*
Hatbox: A Modern Haberdashery
   (p92)
Passport Vintage *(p91)*
Soco Maker's Market *(p104)*
Stag *(p94)*

ARTS & CULTURE

Austin Art Garage *(p121)*
Greetings From Austin *(p128)*
I Love You So Much *(p131)*
Willie For President *(p131)*
ZACH Theatre *(p117)*

NIGHTLIFE

Cidercade Austin *(p157)*
The Continental Club *(p147)*
Ego's *(p159)*
The Golden Goose *(p157)*
Peter Pan Mini-Golf *(p158)*

OUTDOORS

Ann and Roy Butler Hike-and-Bike
   Trail *(p167)*
Austin Runners Club *(p169)*
Zilker Park *(p173)*

0 kilometers 4
0 miles 4

Nina Berenato **S**
N The Rose Room   Blue Starlite
Drive-In

NORTH
AUSTIN   **E** Con Todo

Austin Beerworks **D**
Playland Skate Center **N**   Highland Lanes
N   **S** MT
Daily Juice **D** **N**   Supern
The Original
Pinballz Arcade

Mi Tradición **E**

CRESTVIEW

The Violet Crown **N**
N Vigilante

E Civil Goat

Emma Long
Metropolitan
Park

Covert Park **O**

Mayfield Park and **O**
Nature Preserve

BEE CAVES ROAD

WEST
LAKE HILLS   TARRYTOWN

BARTON
CREEK

Hill of **O**
Life Trail

Deep Eddy Cabaret **D**

See maps 1–5
for Central Austin

Barton Creek **S**
Farmers Market

Barton Creek Greenbelt **O**   BARTON
HILLS

OAK HILL   Soup Peddler **D** **E**   Matt's El
Broken Spoke **N**   Rancho

Radio Coffee & Beer **D**
S
Uncommon Objects   **E** Palo Seco 512

E Plaza
Colombian Coffee Bar   **S** Resistencia
Books

Cathedral of Junk **A**
D St. Elmo Brewing   SOUTHEAST
Company   AUSTIN

The Austin   ST. ELMO   Aust
Winery   Bergst
Interna
Airp

SOUTH
AUSTIN

Lady Bird Johnson **O**
Wildflower Center   McKinney Falls
O State Park

Sam's   Outdoor Yoga **O**
Town Point **N**   **N** The Far Out Lounge

N Giddy Ups

MAP 6

EAT

Matt's El Rancho *(p47)*

Mi Tradición *(p37)*

Plaza Colombian Coffee Bar *(p40)*

Palo Seco 512 *(p49)*

DRINK

Austin Beerworks *(p72)*

The Austin Winery *(p83)*

Civil Goat *(p42)*

Con Todo *(p50)*

Daily Juice *(p67)*

Deep Eddy Cabaret *(p69)*

Live Oak Brewing Company *(p73)*

Radio Coffee & Beer *(p60)*

St. Elmo Brewing Company *(p72)*

Soup Peddler *(p67)*

The Violet Crown *(p81)*

SHOP

Barton Creek Farmers Market *(p98)*

MT Supermarket *(p96)*

Nina Berenato *(p94)*

Resistencia Books *(p101)*

Uncommon Objects *(p88)*

ARTS & CULTURE

Blue Starlite Drive-In *(p119)*

Cathedral of Junk *(p126)*

NIGHTLIFE

Broken Spoke *(p136)*

The Far Out Lounge *(p147)*

Giddy Ups *(p138)*

Highland Lanes *(p156)*

The Original Pinballz Arcade *(p156)*

Playland Skate Center *(p158)*

The Rose Room *(p143)*

Sam's Town Point *(p137)*

Vigilante *(p158)*

OUTDOORS

Barton Creek Greenbelt *(p173)*

Covert Park *(p166)*

Hill of Life Trail *(p164)*

Lady Bird Johnson Wildflower Center *(p175)*

Mayfield Park and Nature Preserve *(p175)*

McKinney Falls State Park *(p172)*

Outdoor Yoga *(p168)*

US-290

Colorado River

Live Oak Brewing Company

TX-71

TX-45

EAT

Tex-Mex is king in Austin, with locals filling up on tacos from breakfast till late. But there's plenty more on the menu – think BBQs, sushi, and even crepes.

Breakfast and Brunch

Brunch – the classic all-American meal – is given a Tex-Mex spin in Austin. And for every order of avocado toast, there's another for tacos (we're talking tortillas stuffed with eggs, meat, and cheese).

EL PRIMO

Map 5; 2011 South 1st Street, Bouldin Creek;
///horizons.submits.canines; www.elprimoatx.com

This rough-and-ready food truck might not look like much, but trust us (and the inevitable line of hungry patrons), it serves up some of the city's tastiest breakfast tacos. Is it worth the wait? You bet. The bacon variety will revolutionize your morning routine. P.S. It's cash only.

BIRD BIRD BISCUIT

Map 3; 2701 Manor Road, Cherrywood; ///hits.altering.partners;
www.birdbirdbiscuit.com

In Texas, a breakfast sandwich should consist of fried chicken wedged between a pillowy biscuit. The best place in Austin to get your hands on this classic dish? Bird Bird Biscuit. The biscuits are fluffy yet flaky, the chicken is spiced and succulent, and it's all covered in either bacon-infused chipotle mayo, basil pesto, or a mind-blowing BBQ sauce.

TAMALE HOUSE EAST

Map 2; 1707 East 6th Street, East Cesar Chavez; ///sheep.fast.kettles; www.tamalehouseeast.com

The Valeras are a culinary dynasty. Carmen and Moses opened the first Tamale House in 1958, serving tamales (cornmeal rolled with ground meat or beans, wrapped in corn husks, and steamed) from a tiny window. Their five children followed suit, becoming restauranteurs, and then *their* children caught the bug, opening Tamale House East in 2012. This generation has added some millennial touches to the business: a plant-filled patio, lengthy cocktail menu, and weekend brunch accompanied by a live jazz band.

» Don't leave without ordering Mom's Migas and Queso (eggs scrambled with pan-fried tortillas, melted cheese, and salsa ranchera).

JOE'S BAKERY

Map 2; 2305 East 7th Street, Central East Austin; ///count.gladiators.dramatic; www.joesbakery.com

Just like the best diners, Joe's Bakery is family-owned and serves breakfast all day, every day. But unlike traditional American joints, Joe's is all about Tex-Mex dishes (this is Austin, after all). Highlights include *pork carne guisada* (slow-cooked pork) and *migas tacos con todo* (tortillas with eggs, corn chips, tomatoes, cheese, and jalapeños).

GRANNY'S TACOS

Map 2; 1401 East 7th Street, Central East Austin;
///nature.bristle.managers; www.grannystacosatx.square.site

If you grew up with a grandmother that could make tacos half as
good as Granny's, you should consider yourself lucky. And if you
didn't, you need to come here. Instead of keeping her grandmother's
cooking to herself, Maria Rios Vega decided to share her *abuela's*
recipes with other Austinites, turning an old ambulance into a taco
truck *in queso* emergencies (sorry). The morning crowd can't get
enough of the egg-and-cactus breakfast tacos and *chilaquiles*
(shredded chicken, cheese, onions, and pickled jalapeños). Both are
topped with a mind-blowing mole sauce that will have you begging
Maria for the recipe.

HILLSIDE FARMACY

Map 2; 1209 East 11th Street, Central East Austin; ///observe.typical.
sharpen; www.hillsidefarmacy.com

We wonder whether director Wes Anderson stumbled upon Hillside
Farmacy as a UT student and took inspiration from its aesthetic.
Based in a 1950s drugstore once run by Doc Young (Austin's first
Black American pharmacist), the exterior is pretty pastel green,
while inside is replete with pentagon-patterned flooring and wooden
cabinets lined with vintage medicine bottles. And although many East
Austinites take visiting friends and relatives here for the setting alone,
they keep coming back for the farm-to-table twists on breakfast
classics. Think Wasabi Bloody Marys and buttermilk pancakes
topped with seasonal fruit from Eastside Urban Farms.

LAUNDERETTE

Map 2; 2115 Holly Street, Holly; ///dweller.relating.riddle;
www.launderetteaustin.com

Housed in – you guessed it – a former laundromat, Launderette is one of the hottest spots for brunch on the East Side. Inside, there isn't a washer or dryer in sight (although the industrial ceiling and linoleum floor are unchanged from its *washateria* days). Instead, a sweeping blue bar and quirky artwork set the scene for groups of friends to catch up over cocktails and creative New American brunch dishes. The menu changes constantly, but the Plancha Burger, a fast-food style patty sandwiched between slices of fluffy challah bread, and topped with a "secret sauce," is a regular fixture. Try it to discover why it's so popular.

» Don't leave without saving room for acclaimed pastry chef Laura Sawicki's birthday-cake ice-cream sandwich, topped with sprinkles. Not your birthday? We won't tell.

Shh!

Marcelino's (*www.marcelinos foods.com*) is named after *Marcelino Pan Y Vino*, an old Mexican folk story that's all about sharing good food. And that's exactly what this scoop-and-serve breakfast taco joint does. Located in a suburban stretch in far East Austin, it's well worth the trek for its offbeat fillings. Think grilled cabbage, squash, and creamed poblanos (a mild Mexican chili). Of course, you can still opt for the classic combo of beans, egg, and bacon, too.

Beloved Bakeries

Those with a sweet tooth will find plenty of dessert spots in Austin. The city is jam-packed with classic bakeries, Mexican panaderia, and vegan cafés serving up plant-based treats.

TEAL HOUSE BAKERY

Map 5; 2304 South Congress Avenue, South Congress;
///fitter.wolf.rings; www.tealhouse.co

The Phillips started selling cinnamon rolls from their teal-painted home to fund a family trip to Disneyland in 2016. Flash-forward to 2020 and their fluffy pastries had garnered such a devoted following that the cottage bakery spawned a food truck and brick-and-mortar store. Here, hungry commuters kick-start their morning with drip coffee and vegan, gluten-free, or gluten-full rolls.

SOUR DUCK MARKET

Map 3; 1814 East Martin Luther King Jr Boulevard, Chestnut;
///crust.wording.pouch; www.sourduckmarket.com

Sour Duck Market is the definition of a neighborhood bakery. Everything is local here: the flour is from Texan millers, the milk is sourced direct from nearby dairies, and the crowd is made up of

Happy hour runs from 3 to 6pm. Show up during this time and Sour Duck will take 20 percent off your bill.

Chestnutters who swear by its 10-year-old starter culture. Some of them even have sourdough subscriptions, picking up freshly baked loaves each day.

MI TRADICIÓN

Map 6; 8716 Research Boulevard #290, Wooten;
///lavender.secretly.items; www.mitradicionbakery.com

Tex-Mex-obsessed Austin is home to countless *panaderias*, so why do people trek out to Wooten for Mi Tradición? Simple: locals know that this place makes the most incredible *conchas* (sweet breads), *pans blanco* (white baguettes), and *tortas* (sandwiches) this side of the border. Everything is handmade here, using traditional methods and recipes. And the bakes taste dang good because of it.

» Don't leave without grabbing some *al pastor* (spit-grilled pork) tacos to go. No judgment if you can't resist gobbling them up right away.

SWEDISH HILL

Map 1; 1120 West 6th Street, Clarksville; ///speaking.printers.singer;
www.swedishhillaustin.com

All it takes is one whiff of the hearth-baked loaves, delicious buns, and flaky pastries for Clarksville residents to pay Swedish Hill a visit. It's as slick a bakery as you'll find in Austin, with a sophisticated menu of comforting bites. Come the weekend, equally stylish locals pop by for their catch-ups – you'd be lucky to find a table free for a quick bite. Takeout it is, then.

LA MEXICANA BAKERY

Map 5; 1924 South 1st Street, Bouldin Creek; ///sends.staging.station;
www.lamexicanabakeryaustin.com

Of course, Austin has a 24-hour Mexican bakery. La Mexicana has
been sating late-night cravings with churros, *chocoflan* (chocolate
cake topped with custard and caramel), and *pan dulce* (sweet
breads) since the early 1990s. So when you have the midnight
munchies, you know where to come.

EASY TIGER

Map 2; 1501 East 7th Street, Central East Austin;
///doctors.protects.bracelet; www.easytigerusa.com

You've probably heard of Easy Tiger – it supplies sourdoughs and
stone-baked ciabattas to some of Austin's best restaurants and
grocers. How's that for endorsement? The bakery has three outposts
in the city, but the East Side Bake Shop and Beer Garden is definitely
our favorite. Here, the after-work crowd feast on freshly baked
pretzels and local beers between games of ping-pong.

Try it!
MAKE YOUR OWN

Obsessed with sourdough? Pick up a
French-style *(levain dur)* starter from Easy
Tiger, which comes with comprehensive
care tips and easy-to-follow recipes. You'll
be baking a loaf in no time at all.

QUACK'S

Map 4; 411 East 43rd Street, Hyde Park; ///barefoot.reveal.folds;
www.quacksbakery.com

Spot the line of sugar-seeking Austinites and you'll know you've arrived at the right place. Quack's is a local household name, once known as the city's first coffee shop before finding fame for its cinnamon rolls, cakes, and cookies (often in vegan incarnations).

COMADRE PANADERÍA

Map 3; 1204 Cedar Avenue, Chestnut; ///deprive.aside.trip;
www.comadrepanaderia.com

You won't come across a bakery as friendly as the pop-up Comdrea Panadería – the name is a nod to friendship, after all. This *panadería* makes Mexican classics with a craft approach. Be quick, though: it's open only on the weekends, and the pastries sell out pretty fast.

ZUCCHINI KILL BAKERY

Map 4; 701 East 53rd Street Suite C, North Loop;
///thunder.visions.coiling; www.zucchinikill.com

The punk-obsessed trio behind Zucchini Kill are uncompromising in their mission to help sweet-toothed Austinites forgo milk, eggs, soy, and gluten. They've given everything from cupcakes to twinkies the vegan treatment and called them music-inspired names like Rebel Swrrrl swiss rolls (a pun on the Bikini Kill song "Rebel Girl").

» Don't leave without checking out the bakery's hearse-turned-delivery van. It doesn't get more punk than that.

Light Bites

Austinites may be known for their love of hearty BBQ and Tex-Mex feasts, but this outdoorsy bunch are equally fond of light and healthy dishes. Life is all about balance, after all.

PLAZA COLOMBIAN COFFEE BAR

Map 6; 3842 South Congress Avenue, Dawson; ///rejects.encoded.castle; www.plazacolombiancoffee.com

Tired of tacos? We'll ignore the sacrilege of that statement and direct you to this Colombian café for *arepas*. These gluten-free corn patties filled with beans, veggies, and cheese, are the perfect healthy snack to eat on the go. If you can resist Plaza's buzzing patio-meets-dancefloor, that is. Here, couples twirl to the live band's Latin beats.

BETTER HALF COFFEE & COCKTAILS

Map 1; 406 Walsh Street, Clarksville; ///royally.keeps.bubbles; www.betterhalfbar.com

With private booths and free Wi-Fi, Better Half is the café of choice for Austin's sizable freelancer community. Every day, they pitch up with their laptops to work on their start-up's business plan while

nursing rosemary lavender lattes and snacking on cauliflower tots.
Come lunchtime, they're joined by local office workers after something light like chilled ramen or vermicelli salad. It's time to say
goodbye to your prepackaged sandwich and day-old leftovers,
and give your lunch an upgrade.

» Don't leave without ordering a frozen cocktail once you've finished
work. We love Whatamelon (watermelon, cucumber, and gin).

BOULDIN CREEK CAFÉ
Map 5; 1900 South 1st Street, Bouldin Creek; ///highs.divided.lays; www.bouldincreekcafe.com

Veggie and vegan out-of-towners rave about Bouldin Creek Café's
tofu scrambled "eggs" and Wanna-BLTA (a vegan BLT) long after
they've gone home. See what all the fuss is about and head here for
a midday mock-meat bite.

JOSEPHINE HOUSE
Map 4; 1601 Waterston Avenue, Clarksville; ///yell.open.paying; www.josephineofaustin.com

A favorite among Austin's well-heeled crowd, Josephine House
oozes Southern charm. It's set in a picture-perfect blue-and-white
Craftsman cottage, complete with a cute outdoor area that you'll
wish was your backyard. And the menu? It's all about comforting
but healthy New American dishes. Think leafy, locally sourced
salads and a rice bowl packed with red rice, pickled vegetables,
sweet red pepper *chimichurri*, and topped with a poached egg.

CIVIL GOAT

Map 6; 704 Cuernavaca Dr, Cuernavaca;
///liver.dolphin.jigsaw; www.civilgoat.com

It takes a lot to outdo the excellent brews here (yes, this is first
and foremost a coffee shop), but the food might just do that.
This popular spot is all about taking it slow and relishing peaceful
moments – and that includes enjoying a brunch bite at any time of
the day. Settle in and order a warm omelette served on a toasted
croissant (and a coffee, of course).

» Don't leave without catching a glimpse of Butters, the shop's very
own Pygmy goat who freely roams around the property.

LENOIR

Map 5; 1807 South 1st Street, Bouldin Creek; ///pulse.lipstick.purple;
www.lenoirrestaurant.com

This is where the Bouldin Creek contingent does date night. Here,
smartly dressed couples split bottles of velvety Côtes du Rhônes and

Shh!

Every Austinite seems to have
a favorite southeast Asian spot,
but not many know about Bodhi
Viet Vegan *(www.bodhiviet
veggies.com)*. Run by Buddhist
nuns and volunteers, this food
truck is a haven for vegans.
Everything on the menu is 100
percent animal-free and, unlike
most plant-based spots, it's
super affordable, too, with
dishes starting at $3.50.

partake in what Lenoir likes to call "Hot Weather Food" – light, fresh, citrusy fare that's perfectly suited to the steamy Texan climate. And on balmy summer evenings, you'd be hard-pressed to find a shadier spot than beneath the 500-year-old oak trees and string lights that frame Lenoir's outdoor "wine garden."

NIXTA

Map 2; 2512 East 12th Street, Rosewood; ///beards.sprawl.exact; www.nixtataqueria.com

Okay, tacos aren't exactly light, but hear us out. At this taqueria, homemade corn tortillas are topped with unconventional fillings: expect the likes of soy-and-citrus-cured tuna crudo, butternut squash, and roasted beet "tartare." The masa and tortillas are more traditional, made fresh on site with corn straight from San Martín Tilcajete, Oaxaca. See – these are tacos on a health-kick.

CASA DE LUZ

Map 5; 1701 Toomey Road, Zilker; ///alive.hops.embedded; www.casadeluz.org

Casa de Luz is not a restaurant. It's a nonprofit community center running yoga, meditation, and wellness classes that also happens to serve vegan, organic, and macrobiotic food, from delicious warming porridge to hearty soups with whole grains. The menus change daily and cover breakfast, lunch, and dinner, making it a perfect stop for a light bite any time of the day. Nourishment for the body and soul? Sign us up.

Comfort Food

Aided by family recipes, Texan chefs are cooking up comfort food like nowhere else – picture Mexican dishes oozing with cheese and pasta piled so high your eyes will pop. So loosen your belt and dig in.

TONY'S JAMAICAN FOOD

Map 2; 1200 East 11th Street, Central East Austin; ///yourself.swim.wasp; (512) 945-5090

East Austin workers have one place in mind for lunch: Tony Scott's food truck. Tony greets them like old friends and loads their plates with authentic Jamaican food that's nothing short of perfection – seriously, try the oxtail; it's heavenly. With reggae music playing in the background and benches offering respite from the blazing sun, it's a real laid-back moment locals never want to end. Sadly, work calls.

FRANKLIN BARBECUE

Map 2; 900 East 11th Street, Central East Austin; ///zoned.risks.sulked; www.franklinbbq.com

This little BBQ joint is an icon on Austin's East Side, known almost as much for its ever-present line as it is for its world-class brisket. Does the line really take all morning? Yep, we won't deny it, but most locals

To ensure you get some brisket, you'll want to show up about 4+ hours prior to opening (11am).

will tell you it's worth it. Set up your camp chairs and bring along some drinks: lining up in the sun with groups of friends is the real Franklin BBQ experience.

MICKLETHWAIT CRAFT MEATS
Map 2; 1309 Rosewood Avenue, Central East Austin;
///rocker.fleet.usual; www.craftmeatsaustin.com

Living in the literal shadow of Franklin Barbecue (they're just down the street), Micklethwait Craft Meats is an unsung BBQ hero. As well as cooking up flawless cuts of brisket and ribs (get ready, they're so dang juicy), this foodie haven is one of the few places where the side dishes are not, contrary to their name, sidelined – expect unique flavors like lemon poppy slaw and a citrus beet salad. And, bonus, you'll be in and out before your buddies over at Franklin even make it through the door.

» Don't leave without trying the banana cream pie. It's a classic dessert that really rounds out a meat-heavy meal.

ASTER'S ETHIOPIAN RESTAURANT
Map 4; 2804 North Interstate Highway 35, Medical District;
///harvest.formally.dart; (512) 469-5966

In need of some serious fuel? UT students know where it's at. When they're deep in exam season, or have that last-minute paper due, they flock to Aster's for lunch. Located right next to campus, this homey spot serves up super-affordable and gorge-worthy vegan *wats* (Ethiopian curries) – ideal for perking up even the most work-weary students.

Solo, Pair, Crowd

Comfort food rules in Austin, so there's plenty of choice for a laid-back meal, whether you're alone or not.

FLYING SOLO
Table for one

Football fan? Then get lost among the crowds at Shoal Creek Saloon, a large and busy sports bar near Downtown. It's a great place to watch games and chow down on some tasty cajun grub.

IN A PAIR
Make a night of it

Looking for a cozy date? Patrizi, right next door to the VORTEX theater, is just the ticket. Tuck into freshly made carbonara before settling in for an evening show.

FOR A CROWD
Start the party

It's always a fiesta at Licha's Cantina, where everything on the "Mexico City soul food" menu is mouthwateringly delicious and the palomas and margaritas flow freely. P.S. Happy hour is 4–6pm Tuesday through Friday.

FONDA SAN MIGUEL

Map 4; 2330 West North Loop Boulevard, Allandale;
///vaccines.degree.troubled; www.fondasanmiguel.com

This stylish restaurant has been representing regional Mexican cuisine for over 45 years. The food's so good, just close your eyes, point at the menu, and you'll end up with something delicious. (Though we can't take responsibility for any strange looks this approach may garner.)

» Don't leave without ordering a watermelon margarita. It's the ultimate refresher on a warm Austin evening.

MATT'S EL RANCHO

Map 6; 2613 South Lamar Boulevard, South Lamar;
///scoring.mugs.behave; www.mattselrancho.com

One day, land commissioner Bob Armstrong walked into this Tex-Mex spot and asked them to make him "something different." The staff promptly whipped up a giant bowl of melted cheese, packed with ground beef and guac, and so the Bob Armstrong queso was born. This hearty dish is legendary all over Texas now – thank you, Bob.

J. LEONARDI'S BARBECUE

Map 2; 1124 East 11th Street, Central East Austin;
///revived.vines.jolly; www.jleonardibbq.com

Austin native Jerome Faulkner comes from BBQ royalty (his heritage of backyard BBQ pitmasters reaches back to the Freedman colonies in the 1870s). No wonder then that his food truck serves up some of the most expertly smoked meat in the city. FYI, portions are hefty.

Taco Trucks

*In a city with nearly as many food trucks as cars,
you're never more than a tortilla's throw away from a
great taco. But locals still have their favorites; here are
some of the top spots they can't get enough of.*

DISCADA

**Map 2; 1319 Rosewood Avenue, Central East Austin;
///desire.exposing.deed; www.discadatx.com**

Indecisives everywhere, rejoice! At Discada, there's only one type of taco, made from a delicious medley of slow-cooked meats with onion, cilantro, and pineapple on top. So the only thing you'll need to decide is how many you can safely put down. Five? Six? Just don't try to keep up with the pro taco-eating Austinites – they're experts, after all.

EL MANA

**Map 3; 1402 East 38th 1/2 Street, Cherrywood;
///wizard.deprive.ships; (512) 662-7208**

El Mana might not look that special from the outside – the low-key food truck is set up in a parking lot between a dry cleaners and a corner store – but there's a reason there's always a line outside. Cheerful owner Norma Flores has quite the fan base in Cherrywood, and not just because she's always great to chat with. Her menu, half printed and half scrawled onto a whiteboard, features favorites like tamales, gorditas, and menudo, plus her super-secret salsa. Do yourself a favor and ask for two servings of the salsa – it might just be the most irresistible item on the menu.

PALO SECO 512

Map 6; 2400 Burleson Road, Oltorf;
///rams.troubled.farmed; (512) 679-0708

If you've ever found yourself mesmerized by videos of cheesy, birria-filled tacos being dunked into a steaming bowl of consommé – they're a thing, don't you know – you'll want to make a visit to Palo Seco 512. The tacos here are packed with flavor, and the consommé is good enough that we've debated whether it's socially acceptable to carry some around in a small hip flask (the jury's still out).

» Don't leave without trying the birria ramen. It's a bowl of Tapatio ramen filled with Palo Seco 512's famous consommé.

ROSITA'S AL PASTOR

Map 3; 1911 East Riverside Drive, Riverside;
///iceberg.fuels.bats; (512) 442-8402

Hunting for a classic Austin taco? There's no better place to go than Rosita's. Timeworn and a touch gritty, this beloved taco joint has been serving its namesake, no-frills tacos since way back in 1985. The place is family-run and has a deeply loyal customer base who often blame them, good-naturedly, for their decades-long taco obsession.

PAPRIKA

Map 4; 6519 North Lamar Boulevard, Highland;
///apricot.motivations.owns; www.paprikaatx.com

This red-hot little truck parked up on North Lamar in 2019 and quickly became a neighborhood favorite. Why? Well, these aren't your normal tacos. Paprika loves to mix it up, so expect tasty variations on traditional fillings – such as *sous vide carnitas* or refried lentil beans.

» Don't leave without trying the homemade green salsa – it's got that perfect citrusy flavor and just the right amount of spice.

CON TODO

Map 6; 10001 Metric Boulevard, North Austin;
///deserved.bridge.gloves; www.contodotacos.com

The Rio Grand Valley-style tacos offered at Con Todo are really something special – good luck finding anywhere else in Austin that serves this south-Texan speciality. You can almost always guarantee a dedicated line of locals here, waiting to get their fix of tacos made with handmade tortillas and using locally sourced ingredients.

CUANTOS TACOS

Map 2; 1108 East 12th Street, Central East Austin;
///presume.else.removes; (512) 903-3918

Tucked away in a low-key food truck park, this tiny taco spot is a magnet for foodies who make a beeline here after work. They're after the Mexico City-style tacos, which are packed full and sell out as fast as they're eaten. Do as the locals do and order more to have later.

Liked by the locals

"The thing that excites me the most about the Austin taco scene is seeing the city show more and more of an appreciation for other tacos besides the ubiquitous breakfast taco. We're excited to be a small part of the Austin taco scene ourselves."

MARGARITO PEREZ, OWNER OF PAPRIKA

Special Occasion

Birthday? Bachelorette party? Bad day? Any and all occasions are marked with a meal in this food-obsessed city. Join locals celebrating their big moments at these memorable spots.

ODD DUCK

Map 5; 1201 South Lamar Boulevard, South Lamar;
///beefed.bumpy.translated; www.oddduckaustin.com

It's a story you'll hear many times in this city: a food truck generates a thunderstorm of hype and quickly becomes a brick-and-mortar. Just look at Odd Duck. Brothers and owners Bryce and Dylan Gilmore used local ingredients in their pork sliders, and Austinites went wild for them. Today, Odd Duck's a little bit more fancy (think scallops and wagyu beef), but it's still committed to farm-to-table cooking.

COMEDOR

Map 1; 501 Colorado Street, Downtown; ///lists.finally.force;
www.comedortx.com

Good ol' fashioned Mexican cooking gets a chic new makeover at this date-night staple. The standout dish? The bone marrow tacos, which cuddled-up couples assemble at the table, topping tortillas with

After dinner, head next door to Garage. It's a speakeasy-style lounge located in, well, a parking garage.

salty greens, smoked butter, bone marrow, and a pecan gremolata – you won't find these tacos at a truck. Make a reservation for your next anniversary.

MUSASHINO

**Map 4; 2905 San Gabriel Street Suite 200, Heritage;
///divide.stumpy.grazed; www.musashinoatx.com**

Although far away from the nearest coast, Austin has become known as a sushi town. And Musashino has played a big part in its reputation. This is where many of the city's top chefs, like Uchi's Tyson Cole and Ramen Tatsu-ya's Tatsu Aikawa and Takuya Matsumoto, started out. But despite its fame, Musashino is surprisingly laid-back on the whole – there's no need to make a reservation months in advance and the menu is semi-affordable (this is sushi, after all).

OLAMAIE

**Map 4; 1610 San Antonio Street, Campus; ///bedroom.weaved.vertical;
www.olamaieaustin.com**

College kids love fast food, so it's really not surprising that Campus is awash with quick-service restaurants. But among the chains is this upscale Southern spot. Come graduation time, students bring their parents here to celebrate over Carolina Gold rice hush puppies (fried rice balls) and Hoppin' Johns (black-eyed peas and rice).

» Don't leave without asking your server for some biscuits. They're a not-so-secret off-menu item that you don't want to miss.

Solo, Pair, Crowd

Whatever the occasion or group size, there are plenty of places to treat yourself to a special meal in Austin.

FLYING SOLO
Sake and sushi
Nothing says self-care like a sushi lesson at Uroko. Learn how to roll your own with talented chefs Takehiro Azazu and Masazumi Saio, while you sip sake and chat with your fellow sushi enthusiasts.

IN A PAIR
Treat for two
Split a plate of cold-water oysters at the ever-romantic Clark's Oyster Bar in Clarksville. They pair well with a dry martini.

FOR A CROWD
Variety for vegans
Austin's first-ever vegan gastropub, The Beer Plant accompanies shareable plant-based dishes with over 40 different beers from local breweries. Bring the gang (even the ardent carnivores) and enjoy a healthy evening – kinda. How virtuous can a beer-fueled event really be?

KEMURI TATSU-YA

Map 2; 2713 East 2nd Street, Holly; ///splendid.station.booster;
www.kemuri-tatsuya.com

Looking for somewhere different to celebrate your birthday? It doesn't get more unique than this BBQ-*izakaya* hybrid. Surrounded by Texan taxidermy and Japanese signage, your party can share the likes of chili cheese *takoyaki* (octopus balls) and BBQ bento boxes.

» Don't leave without trying a Matcha Painkiller. It's Kemuri's take on the classic rum cocktail, served in a cute cat-shaped glass.

JUSTINE'S

Map 3; 4710 East 5th Street, Govalle; ///romance.scrap.lucky;
www.justines1937.com

This sexy, late-night brasserie attracts a steady stream of trendy people looking to splurge their paychecks. Low lighting, deep-red walls, and antique mirrors create a swish vibe, which is matched by decadent French dishes like buttery escargot, steak tartare, and moules frites.

VIXEN'S WEDDING

Map 2; 1813 East 6th Street, East Cesar Chavez;
///client.mushroom.handbook; www.vixensweddingatx.com

With its bright-blue chairs, hanging lamps, and plants, this hotel restaurant is picture-perfect. Glam friends flock here for swanky dinners in the pretty space, snapping photos left, right, and center for their social media. The Goan menu is just as enticing – this is regional Indian food done right.

A day on the taco trail in
East Austin

Did we mention that Austinites love tacos? Originally hailing from south of the border, this Tex-Mex dish is emblematic of Austin's historic and cultural connection to Mexico. Historically home to the city's Mexican American community, East Austin is the best place to experience Mexican American culture, hopping between the neighborhood's many taco trucks and *taquerias*, museums, and cultural centers.

Top off at
TORCHY'S TACOS
What was once a tiny trailer has spawned brick-and-mortar outposts across the city. Pop by this branch to get your taco fix and be sure to order *elotes* (chargrilled corn on the cob).

WEST 12TH ST

WEST AVE

3 EAST 2

Butler Metro Park

SOUTH 1ST STREET

SOUTH CON

SOUTH CON

1. Granny's Tacos
1401 East 7th Street, Central East Austin; www.grannys tacosatx.square.site
///nature.bristle.managers

2. Mexic-Arte Museum
419 Congress Avenue, Downtown; www. mexic-artemuseum.org
///reef.probably.dent

3. Torchy's Tacos
110 San Antonio Street, Downtown; www.torchys tacos.com
///wriggle.martini.resolved

4. Emma S. Barrientos Mexican American Cultural Center
600 River Street, Rainey; (512) 974-3772
///emails.volcano.costumes

5. Las Trancas
1210 East Cesar Chavez Street, East Cesar Chavez; (512) 701-8287
///share.tailors.broads

📍 **Teatro Vivo**
///emails.volcano.costumes

📍 **Texas State Cemetery**
///couch.quit.roofer

Oakwood
Cemetery

EAST 15TH STREET

Texas State
Capitol

CENTRAL EAST
AUSTIN

Waller Creek

EAST 11TH STREET

I-35

US settlers and Tejanos
(Texan Mexicans) who
fought in the 1835 Texas
Revolution against
Mexico are buried in the
Texas State Cemetery.

DOWNTOWN

EAST 7TH STREET

WEST 5TH ST

2

Swing by the
MEXIC-ARTE MUSEUM

Work up an appetite as
you check out sculpture,
installations, and paintings
from beyond the border.

EAST 7TH STREET

EAST CESAR
CHAVEZ

ATTAYAC STREET

Fortify yourself at
GRANNY'S TACOS

Start your day the Austin
way with a classic
breakfast taco. Expect
fillings like *chicharrón*
(fried pork), slathered in
a mole sauce.

1

*Located in the Mexican
American Cultural
Center, Teatro Vivo is
Texas's only bilingual
English-Spanish
theater company.*

EAST CESAR
CHAVEZ ST

Colorado River

4

RIVER ST

HOLLY STREET

WALLER STREET

5

Finish up at
LAS TRANCAS

Still hungry? Stop for a
couple of tacos at this
late-night taco truck. It's
just as busy at noon as
midnight, when the post-
party crowds stream in.

EAST CESAR CHAVEZ ST

Join a class at the
MMA S. BARRIENTOS
MEXICAN AMERICAN
CULTURAL CENTER

Get your hands dirty
while learning how to
grow traditional Mexican
healing herbs. These plants
pep up even the most
everyday recipes.

I-35

0 meters	500
0 yards	500

DRINK

Locals spend a lot of time on patios, soaking up the Texan sun and listening to live music while quaffing coffee, craft beers, or happy-hour cocktails.

Coffee Shops

Austinites know how to get their caffeine fix. The city is replete with cutting-edge roasters and espresso gurus. And because this is Austin we're talking about, there's almost always a sun-drenched patio involved.

FIGURE 8 COFFEE PURVEYORS

Map 2; 1111 Chicon Street, Blackshear-Prospect Hill; ///curated.defended.skewed; www.figure8coffeepurveyors.com

In a city of start-ups and side hustlers, a coffee shop that started out as a side project by some of the city's best baristas is sure to draw a like-minded crowd. Silicon Hills workers love Figure 8, tapping away on laptops in its plant-filled interior, while nursing *cortados* and cappuccinos made from roasts described as having a "velvety body" or "vibrant acidity." Who said only wine had tasting notes?

RADIO COFFEE & BEER

Map 6; 4204 Manchaca Road, South Lamar; ///boil.offshore.paper; www.radiocoffeeandbeer.com

Radio is one of those places where you could feasibly spend an entire day (and people often do). The Wi-Fi is fast and free; there are three on-site food trucks serving up tacos, Thai, and more for

The best time to visit Radio is on Monday nights, when world-class string players jam out on stage. when you get peckish; and there's always something going on in the evening – from ultra-nerdy trivia nights to bluegrass jams. Oh, and there's coffee, of course.

GREATER GOODS

Map 2; 2501 East 5th Street, Holly; ///incoming.insect.routines; www.greatergoodsroasting.com

The espresso here comes with a complimentary feel-good glow. And no, it's not just the caffeine. The beans are sourced from sustainable producers who pay their workers fairly, the on-site "training lab" educates aspiring baristas in how to source green coffee, and Greater Goods donates to one of four nonprofits with each cup or bag of coffee sold. A latte that supports a good cause? Order us a cup.

DESNUDO COFFEE

Map 3; 32505 Webberville Road, East Austin; ///sorted.back.armed; www.desnudocoffee.com

It's easy to spot this micro-trailer coffee joint, located in a food truck park, given the lines snaking around the block. But don't let that put you off – it's simply a sign of just how much the brothers who run it have won over the hearts of Austinites with their friendly service and menu of unique brews. The best part? All of the coffee used is sustainably sourced direct from small coffee farms.

» **Don't leave without** trying one of the deliciously mixed coffees; our favorite is the miso brown sugar latte.

Solo, Pair, Crowd

Whether you're after a single shot of espresso or on a languorous date, Austin has a coffee shop for you.

FLYING SOLO
Pit stop espresso
In Italian style, frequenters of Fleet Coffee find themselves shoulder to shoulder in a shoebox-size space. If fast friends and good espresso are your thing, there are few locations that can rival this one.

IN A PAIR
Coffee to craft beer
Wright Bros. Brew & Brew has you covered if you're looking for a catch-all date spot. Here, a casual coffee meetup can seamlessly slide into a beer-fueled evening. If things are going well, that is.

FOR A CROWD
A groovy gathering
Gather the gang for a day on Spider House Ballroom's patio, where cups of Joe come with a side of unconventional events. Think poetry slams, drunk spelling bees, and VHS swap meets.

CUVÉE COFFEE

Map 2; 2000 East 6th Street, Holly; ///successes.cabinets.nodded;
www.cuveecoffee.com

With a strictly enforced no-laptop, no-Wi-Fi policy, this micro-roastery-meets-coffee-shop forces you to get off your devices and appreciate the roast. Which is ironic given that Cuvée uses the latest technology to custom dial its beans and can its nitro cold brews.

EPOCH COFFEE

Map 4; 221 West North Loop Boulevard, North Loop;
///powerful.stereos.social; www.epochcoffee.com

Art and coffee come together at Epoch. No, we're not talking about latte art – although the baristas can create a mean design. This coffeehouse supports local artists by exhibiting and selling their work. No wonder creatives flock here to put the finishing touches to their novels, screenplays, and sketches.

CHERRYWOOD COFFEEHOUSE

Map 3; 1400 East 38th 1/2 Street, Cherrywood;
///elaborate.district.universally; www.cherrywoodcoffeehouse.com

An off-duty chef reading the paper. A pair of coworkers catching up over coffee and breakfast tacos. The Texan politician Beto O'Rourke (he's hosted a fundraiser here). Cherrywood's devoted crowd of regulars reflects all walks of Austin life.

» Don't leave without checking out what's on on the tree-shaded patio – there might be music, stand-up, or trivia.

Juice and Smoothie Bars

In a city as mind- and body-conscious as this one, it's little wonder that locals love juices and smoothies. After yoga, hiking, or stand-up paddleboarding, they crave these hydrating and healthy beverages.

MR. NATURAL

Map 2; 1901 East Cesar Chavez Street, East Cesar Chavez; ///panel.courage.solids; www.mrnatural-austin.com

When Jesus and Maria moved to Texas from Mexico in the late 1990s, they brought with them their passion for all things healthy – and their grandmothers' recipes. Enjoy *abuela*'s yummy juices, smoothies, and *agua frescas* at this vegan eatery-health store hybrid.

REVOLUCIÓN COFFEE + JUICE

Map 1; 207 San Jacinto Blvd Suite 200, Downtown; ///pinches.smarter.forks; www.revolucionsa.com

Originally hailing from San Antonio, this juice bar has made a splash in nearby Austin. A buck may not stretch far in this stylish spot, but what it lacks in bargains, it makes up for in quality drinks.

Not sure what to order? Try a "juice flight": eight, 2 oz (60 ml) servings of varied juice blends.

The selection of juices are cold-pressed and blended to suit various tastes and needs, meaning you get maximum plant power out of every sip.

BLENDERS & BOWLS

Map 2; 1625 East 6th Street, East Cesar Chavez; ///estimate.sofa.able; www.blendersandbowls.com

After a summer spent surfing and snacking on acai bowls in Hawaii, BFFs Erin and Kara decided to introduce Austin to their new fave flavor. They set up a food truck, serving bowls like the Dream Boat (acai, berries, and vanilla almond milk), which soon turned brick-and-mortar and spawned a nationwide grocery line of frozen smoothies.

LA FRUTA FELIZ

Map 3; 3124 Manor Road, MLK; ///stables.pleasing.trace; www.lafrutafeliz.com

We're not really sure if La Fruta Feliz is a juice shop that also makes excellent tacos, or a taqueria with a great selection of juices. Either way, this no-frills strip-mall spot excels at all things Mexican. For a taste of life across the border, pull up a chair, grab a *horchata* (rice milk) or melon *aguas fresca* (melon blended with water and lime juice), and, if you know your Spanish, keep an ear out for local gossip. (We've heard there's karaoke on Sunday mornings.)

» Don't leave without grabbing some carb-loaded *barbacoa de chivo* (braised goat) tacos. Life is all about balance, right?

PEOPLE'S PHARMACY

Map 4; 4018 North Lamar Boulevard, North Lamar;
///flops.habit.sharper; www.peoplespharmacy.com

The healthiest juice in town? It's a hard-fought title, but we reckon People's Pharmacy is in with a good shot. This literal pharmacy mixes up organic smoothies and prepares cold-pressed juices with the same care and attention as its medicines. (Don't worry: they're made in the on-site deli rather than the lab.) An apple, avocado, pineapple, and mango a day keep the doctor away, right?

JUICELAND

Map 5; 1625 Barton Springs Road, Zilker; ///blossom.clouds.liners;
www.juiceland.com

Self-confessed hippie Matt Shook became obsessed with smoothies and juices when he tried a hemp-laced one after a dip at Barton Springs. His passion soon turned into 20-plus JuiceLand outposts in Austin alone, including the OG location around the corner from where Shook's passion started: Barton Springs. But despite his

Try it!
TAKE A YOGA CLASS

Yoga and juice – they just go together. Fortunately, Juiceland is just around the corner from the Umlauf Sculpture Garden, which hosts outdoor classes (www.umlaufsculpture.org/yoga).

mini-empire, Shook holds onto his values. Everything is sustainable, the company donates to nonprofits, and you'll find CBD and hemp in plenty of the concoctions.

SOUP PEDDLER

Map 6; 2801 South Lamar Boulevard, South Lamar; ///doing.emperor.fall; www.souppeddler.com

Whenever Austin gets a little bit of rain, or the temperature drops below 70 degrees, it seems like half of the city makes a dash to Soup Peddler for a comforting bowl of something warm. The rest of the time, they're here for the large selection of cold-pressed juices and smoothies. Try one of their cleverly named blends – like the Seven Veggie Army (carrot, beet, celery, spinach, parsley, cabbage, and kale) or Pulp Friction (grapefruit, orange, pineapple, lemon, lime) – or customize your own one. Good luck coming up with the name.

» Don't leave without grabbing an extra soup to go. It keeps and reheats well, so you can save it for the next cold day.

DAILY JUICE

Map 6; 8620 Burnet Road, North Shoal Creek; ///central.connects.soldiers; www.dailyjuicecafe.com

Say no to pasteurized store-bought juices and opt for a Daily Juice instead. Health-conscious Austinites love this raw, cold-pressed juice brand, swinging by its café to grab a juice, smoothie, or slice of "garden toast," made from dehydrated sunflower and flaxseeds, and topped with the likes of hemp seeds, pickled red onion, and walnut "meat."

Neighborhood Bars

*Every Austinite argues that their local watering hole
is the best: it has the cheapest beer, the coolest vibe,
and the hottest patio. So who's right? Check out
these places to find your favorite.*

NICKEL CITY

**Map 2; 1133 East 11th Street, Central East Austin; ///graced.tiny.mentions;
www.nickelcitybar.com**

Combining the stylish interior and drinks menu of a cocktail bar with
the friendly, faithful crowd of a neighborhood dive, Nickel City is
always a popular post-work choice – especially on hump days,
when locals flock here for Whiskey Wednesdays tastings.

» Don't leave without ordering some sliders and wings from Delray
Cafe, aka "the food truck behind Nickel City."

CROWN & ANCHOR PUB

**Map 4; 2911 San Jacinto Boulevard, Campus; ///social.gent.stunning;
www.crownandanchorpub.com**

It might sound like an old-fashioned boozer from across the pond,
but the Crown & Anchor is an all-American watering hole. It
specializes in Texan beer, with over 30 on tap, and countless more

bottled and canned; has a ton of pool tables and dartboards; and plays endless football games on its five big screens. Oh, and it has a five-hour daily "happy hour." Welcome to Texas, y'all. But, naturally, this is Texas, Austin-style: expect a huge dog-friendly patio, yummy veggie burgers, and some excellent nonalcoholic IPAs thrown into the mix.

DEEP EDDY CABARET

Map 6; 2315 Lake Austin Boulevard, Old West Austin;
///muddle.treaties.drainage; www.deepeddycabaret.com

Founded in 1951, Deep Eddy Cabaret is an honest-to-goodness neighborhood dive, with none of the glitz of the newer, hipper incarnations. Here, grizzled regulars gather underneath the year-round Christmas lights to guzzle cheap pitchers of Lone Star, play a few rounds of pool, and spin Willie Nelson tunes on the jukebox.

Shh!

In the pitch-dark basement of the 120-year-old Goodman building right next to the Capitol, you'll find one of the most covert, cavelike bars in the city: The Cloak Room. Rumor has it that, when the Texas legislature is in session, under-the-table dealings get made here. We don't know if that's true, but you're sure to spot an off-duty politician or two reflecting on the business of the day. Despite the high-profile crowd, expect a laid-back vibe and cheap drinks.

KINDA TROPICAL

Map 3; 3501 East 7th Street, Govalle; ///prance.surgical.stared;
www.kindatropical.com

When the mercury soars, mates and dates flock to Kinda Tropical
for some vacation vibes. The interior is distinctly Caribbean, the
large patio looks kinda like a beach, and the crowd is clad in loud
Hawaiian shirts. And the refreshments? Think piña coladas and
frozen mango margs topped with boozy ice pops. If that isn't
enough to chill you out, try some CBD waffles.

C-BOYS HEART & SOUL

Map 5; 2008 South Congress Avenue, South Congress;
///rocks.trails.decades; www.cboys.com

Skip the weekend chickens*** bingo (it's more of a hit with out-of-
towners than locals anyway) and hit up C-Boys during the week for
some fantastic live music. Take your pick from swing on Tuesdays,
reggae on Thursdays, and soul on Fridays.

» Don't leave without checking out the Jade Room upstairs. This
swanky and sexy lounge is modeled on a 1950s Japanese GI bar.

DRINKS LOUNGE

Map 3; 2001 East Cesar Chavez St, East Cesar Chavez;
///themes.december.funnels; www.drinksrecords.com

Drinks and music go together like rhythm and blues, and no local
dive bar brings them together quite like Austin's Drinks Lounge. In
the bar area, there are usually groups of locals hanging out over

causal drinks – there's everything from local beers to cocktails that really hit the spot. In a cozy side room, there's a whole record store to explore with an awesome vinyl selection, as well as some music memorabilia. Head in for a chill drink, head out the proud new owner of a rare LP.

THE HOLE IN THE WALL

Map 4; 2538 Guadalupe Street, The Drag; ///lied.slug.tugging; www.holeinthewallaustin.com

Since 1974, this small space has served up two things: ice-cold Lone Star beer and great music. Generations of beginner bands, established touring acts, and famous rock stars – like Lucinda Williams, Stevie Ray Vaughan, and Nanci Griffith – have performed here for the loyal locals. Expect a mix of college students and long-time residents, and don't be surprised if you see that actor in that thing shooting some pool on the table beside you.

BARFLY'S

Map 4; 5420-B, Airport Boulevard, Highland; ///sushi.herds.tropic; www.barflysaustin.com

Look up the words "dive bar" in the dictionary and you just might see a picture of Barfly's. Located on soulless Airport Boulevard, this windowless joint is located up a super-steep set of stairs. So why do locals love it? The drinks are shockingly stiff, the jukebox plays obscure rock and indie gems, and everyone knows each other. It's basically a much cooler version of Cheers.

Beer Bars and Breweries

Locals will tell you a refreshing brew is an essential
during Austin's long hot summers. And with more
breweries than any city in Texas, you'll have plenty
of places to choose from if you need cooling down.

AUSTIN BEERWORKS
Map 6; 3001 Industrial Terrace, North Burnet;
///twirls.cheater.cave; www.austinbeerworks.com

Sure, you can get Austin Beerworks' colorful cans all over town, but locals know to come to the source for the good stuff – i.e.,limited edition beers. Join Austinites of all ages (and their dogs) on this brewery's patio for a laid-back evening under the fairy lights.

ST. ELMO BREWING COMPANY
Map 6; 440 East St. Elmo Road G-2, St. Elmo;
///asleep.zones.tweaked; www.stelmobrewing.com

There are a lot of things to love about St. Elmo. The brewery's large, the patio's spacious, and there's ample room inside should the sun prove the victor on a hot afternoon. But our favorite thing might just be the kolsch – the crisp German beer is one of the best in town, and one of the single most refreshing beers you'll find in Austin. Oh, and there's also a great food truck here serving fried chicken with a southeast Asian twist – trust us, it's the perfect combo with a good brew.

LIVE OAK BREWING COMPANY

Map 6; 1615 Crozier Lane, Airport; ///lizard.drainage.wing; www.liveoakbrewing.com

Picture this: benches sprawled under a shady oak tree grove, with the soothing trickle of the Colorado River in the distance. Sound idyllic? Austin's 20- and 30-somethings think so. Live Oak, located in the leafy suburbs, is their destination of choice when the scorching sun forces them to escape the city center. They'll head here in the early afternoon and spend the next few hours sipping European-style beer beneath the trees. A few drinks down, someone will probably suggest a game of disc golf (there's a full-size course here, so it's pretty hard to resist).

» Don't leave without trying a fresh-baked pretzel or some schnitzel from the on-site food truck. It's some of the best German food in town.

Try it!
BIKE FOR YOUR BEER

Take a cycling tour of Austin's wide array of craft breweries with Bike and Brew ATX (www.bikeandbrewatx.com). Rides vary in location, duration, and difficulty, so all are welcome.

BANGER'S

Map 1; 79 Rainey Street, Rainey;

///award.coasted.spits; www.bangersaustin.com

With its prime Rainey Street location and its 200-tap beer list, this lively spot certainly draws quite the crowd – so don't be surprised if there's a wait for one of the beer garden tables. But with a bit of patience, you'll find yourself met with one of the largest draft beer lists in the state. There's also live music on the weekend – bangin'.

PINTHOUSE PIZZA

Map 4; 4729 Burnet Road, Brentwood;

///nibbles.frame.suitcase; www.pinthousepizza.com

Out-of-towners are often surprised to hear that one of the best IPAs in Austin is brewed at a pizzeria – locals aren't; they know their city is anything but ordinary. It's no accident, though, the guys who run the

Shh!

Beer fans looking to try something truly unique should visit next-door neighbors Batch Craft Beer & Kolaches *(www. batchatx.com)* and Oddwood Ales *(www.oddwoodales.com)*. These two breweries are quietly fermenting some of the most creative brews in town. While Oddwood specializes in light and refreshing IPAs, Batch's selection is more whimsical, with specialties like a hibiscus pilsen malt making an appearance alongside a Mexican hot chocolate stout.

place just love craft brews as much as they love pizza. The beers here, all nautically named – we're not sure why – cover a range of styles, from the Bearded Seal dry Irish stout to the super-popular Electric Jellyfish IPA. Try a flight until you land on a favorite, and don't forget to grab a pizza to go with it, too.

» Don't leave without purchasing a special crowler (a giant can) of your favorite brew to drink later.

DRAUGHT HOUSE PUB & BREWERY
Map 4; 4112 Medical Parkway, Rosedale;
///copes.tigers.disposal; www.draughthouse.com

Located in a Tudor-style building, this spot – not too dissimilar to an old English pub – has been serving great beer since it opened in the 1960s. Low-key regulars have been coming here for years, but more recently, Draught House has grabbed the attention of a new crowd. Why? Younger Austinites have discovered the beer list: over 70 local and international drafts (some even brewed in-house).

THE AUSTIN BEER GARDEN BREWING CO.
Map 5; 1305 West Oltorf Street, South Lamar;
///scouts.digress.fines; www.theabgb.com

If the constant accolades and three-time "brewpub of the year" awards at the Great American Beer Festival weren't enough to convince you to stop in to The ABGB for a drink, maybe the excellent *muffaletta* or the prosciutto-and-pesto pizza will do the trick. Bring all your friends – the long benches here are the perfect spot for a party.

Cocktail Joints

Austinites may be a fairly casual crowd, but they still can't resist the lure of a fancy drinking joint. You won't find any rowdy watering holes on this list – serious cocktail connoisseurs only, y'all.

ROOSEVELT ROOM

Map 1; 307 West 5th Street, Downtown/Warehouse District;
///rivers.packages.reserved; www.therooseveltroomatx.com

It might not look like much from the outside (dark bricks and an old metal door don't yell fancy), but once you're inside this Downtown hangout, you'll get the hype. Pairing a cool, industrial-chic interior with a creative menu of cocktails means the place is buzzing with young professionals every evening. New to the craft cocktail hype? Ask the knowledgeable bartenders; they're always happy to assist.

HERE NOR THERE

Map 1; 612 Brazos Street, Downtown;
///graver.mainland.giggled; www.hntaustin.com

Austin's worst-kept secret is a semi-private speakeasy-style bar – and requires a bit of a hunt to find the entrance (it's down the alleyway, shh). If you're lucky enough to make it in, you're in for a real treat.

Here Nor There happily welcomes nonmembers, but you'll have to book through its app.

Expect experimental, and delicious, cocktails served to small groups of friends and couples in dimly lit booths. Intimate date night, done.

MIDNIGHT COWBOY

Map 1; 313 East 6th Street, Downtown;
///ponies.divider.primary; www.midnightcowboymodeling.com

Hidden in the heart of Dirty Sixth (Austin's notorious drinking district), Midnight Cowboy is one of the oldest speakeasies in Austin, and its history is, shall we say, colorful. The bar was once a brothel masquerading as a massage parlor – in fact, a sign proclaiming "Midnight Cowboy Modeling Oriental Massage" still stands. It's reservations-only at this now exclusive cocktail den, where bar-goers sip potent Prohibition-era drinks and sink into the tufted-leather booths.

WATERTRADE

Map 5; 1603 South Congress Avenue, South Congress;
///speech.safari.informed; www.otokoaustin.com/watertrade

It's all about the custom-made cocktails at this swanky bar, tucked away in the Otoko hotel. Simply relax on the designer furniture and give the bartender full control over your order. The result? A world-class cocktail created using seasonal ingredients and fine Japanese spirits. It'll be totally unique – so be prepared to try anything.

» Don't leave without sampling bar bites from the limited *izakaya*-style menu, which was helmed by local culinary genius Yoshi Okai.

Solo, Pair, Crowd

Sipping solo? On a date? Out with your crew? There's a cocktail den for every kind of party in Austin.

FLYING SOLO
Read all about it
It's all about the three Bs at The Wheel: a bike, a brew, and a good book. Chill on the outside patio at this bicycle-inspired bar with your latest read and a low-key cocktail.

IN A PAIR
A secret speakeasy
Small Victory is one of the hardest-to-find bars in Austin (on purpose – it's a speakeasy in an unmarked parking garage), which makes for a fab date-night adventure. Once you're in, the vintage cocktails and intimate atmosphere make the hunt well worth it.

FOR A CROWD
Have a drink with the cool kids
With the gang? It's got to be Whisler's. This rustic-chic neighborhood haunt is where all the cool people hang. If it's a weekend, don't miss checking out Mezcaleria Tobala, the Oaxacan-style mezcal bar upstairs.

GARAGE

Map 1; 503 Colorado Street, Downtown;
///fees.balance.facing; www.garagetx.com

Blink and you'll miss it. Garage is tucked away in a (you guessed it) literal parking garage. This is one of Austin's most elusive bars, with bartenders churning out expertly crafted cocktails inside a moody space that you'd never be able to discern from its exterior. Expect a savvy crowd of "secret" bar-seeking hipsters who relish a scene.

HALF STEP

Map 1; 75 ½ Rainey Street, Rainey; ///hormones.insist.hinders;
www.pouringwithheart.com/half-step

When work ends, techies have one place in mind for drinks: Half Step's lively patio. You'll probably overhear more chats about cryptocurrency and biohacking at this laid-back bar than you're comfortable with, but the cocktail menu, plus regular live music, is worth sticking around for.

» Don't leave without telling your bartender what you like and letting them concoct a special cocktail, just for you.

KITTY COHEN'S

Map 2; 2211 Webberville Road #3548, Central East Austin;
///cabin.dodges.singing; www.kittycohens.com

A Palm Springs-inspired oasis, Kitty Cohen's is the place to be on a sultry evening in Austin. The vibe is pure retro-tropical here – we're talking flamingo wallpaper, palm trees, dangerously tasty drinks, and even a patio with a small wading pool (don't worry; it's adults only).

Wine Bars and Wineries

The Texas Hill Country wineries are second only to Napa Valley's, so it should come as no surprise that Austinites like to drink local, organic, and natural at any given opportunity.

LOLO

Map 2; 1504 East 6th Street, East Cesar Chavez; ///hers.embedded.feed; www.lolo.wine

One of Austin's first dedicated natural wine bars, LoLo is *the* place to really understand organic farming and low-intervention wine-making techniques. The friendly staff wax poetic about processes, flavors, and notes before pouring you a glass.

HOUSE WINE

Map 5; 408 Josephine Street, Zilker; ///crisper.park.necklace; www.housewineaustin.com

Walking into House Wine will instantly make you feel, well, at home (it's in a converted house, after all, complete with hanging plants and pink couches). And as this is Austin, where outdoor living rules

On Sundays, House Wine serves up a budget-friendly selection of half-priced glasses and bottles.

for much of the year, there's a covered patio out back, with twinkling lights and acoustic performances. You might as well order a bottle – you'll be here a while.

AVIARY WINE & KITCHEN

Map 5; 2110 South Lamar Boulevard, South Lamar;
///racing.glades.sublime; www.aviarywinekitchen.com

With its funky bar stools and globular hanging lights, it won't come as a surprise that Aviary started off life as a home goods store. Internet shopping (Amazon, we're looking at you) put an end to the boutique, but a Kickstarter campaign launched this wine bar in its place. And, boy, are the folks of Austin glad. Join them over charcuterie boards and wines from the Jayne Mansfield (rosés), David Bowie (bubbles), or Robin Williams (lively reds) lists.

THE VIOLET CROWN

Map 6; 7100 Woodrow Ave, Crestview;
///stealing.occurs.bonnet; www.thevioletcrownatx.com

The Violet Crown may be a coffee shop full of remote workers by day, but, come evening, laptops on the tables are swapped for wine glasses. Locals shoot the breeze over a bottle (or two) from the selection of US and international natural wines from smaller wineries, lending the spot a real neighborhood feel.

» Don't leave without trying some of the small bites – the oysters here go down a treat.

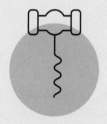

Liked by the locals

"This is the most rewarding time to be in the Texas wine scene. We've been early flag bearers of Texas wine and low-intervention winemaking, and now both are having a moment in the sun – we are really thankful for it!"

ROSS MCLAUCHLAN, OWNER OF THE AUSTIN WINERY

THE AUSTIN WINERY

Map 6; 440 East St. Elmo Road A1, St. Elmo;
///rooster.smoker.camera; www.theaustinwinery.com

You won't find any vines at this urban winery. Instead, the young team of winemakers use grapes from across Texas to create its vintages. The list leans heavily on low-intervention varieties, but it also features plenty of piquettes, field blends, and skin-contact orange wines.

APT 115

Map 2; 2025 East 7th Street, Holly; ///useful.outwit.diary;
www.apartmentonefifteen.com

Mismatched trinkets, a retro TV, a bookcase: APT 115 has really committed to its apartment-complex setting. And with space for only 20 at a time, plus the soundtrack of owner and musician Joe Pannenbacker's vinyl collection, it's got a house party vibe to match.

» Don't leave without opting for a small bite from the wine bar menu — you can never go wrong with a good cheese board.

JUNE'S ALL DAY

Map 5; 1722 South Congress Avenue, South Congress;
///views.purely.magnets; www.junesallday.com

A bar named after one of Texas's few master sommeliers (June Rodil) is bound to have an epic wine list. And June's All Day doesn't disappoint. The team selects a fresh roster of by-the-glass options each month based on a theme, such as "Women of Wine" and "Island Wines to Beat the Heat." Pour us a glass.

An evening on
South Congress

Standing toe-to-toe with music legend Willie Nelson in the battle for Austin's most beloved resident are the Mexican free-tailed bats that roost under Congress Bridge – and their twilight flight is one of Austin's most iconic sights. After you've watched this nighttime spectacle, join the locals on the daily bar hop along South Congress Avenue (or SoCo as it's known). All the best representations of Austin's bar scene are found on this street: old-school dives and trendy wine bars, craft beers and crafted cocktails.

1. Congress Avenue Bridge
Congress Avenue Bridge, South Congress;
///clocked.join.upset

2. Watertrade
1603 South Congress Avenue, South Congress;
www.otokoaustin.com/watertrade
///speech.safari.informed

3. June's All Day
1722 South Congress Avenue, South Congress;
www.junesallday.com
///views.purely.magnets

4. Ego's
510 South Congress Avenue, South Congress;
(512) 474-7091
///fork.blend.speaking

The Continental Club
///swatted.puddles.revolts

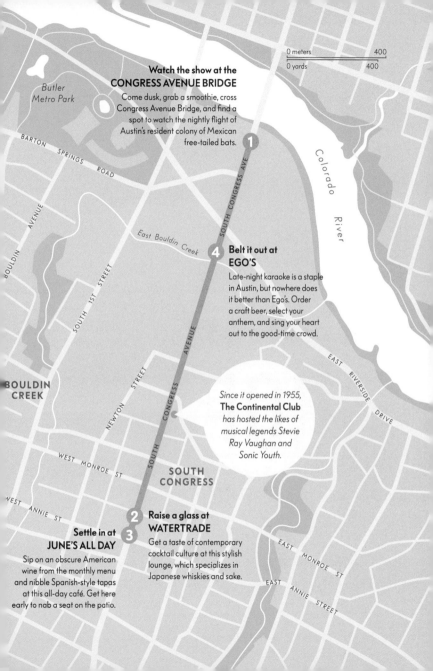

Watch the show at the CONGRESS AVENUE BRIDGE

Come dusk, grab a smoothie, cross Congress Avenue Bridge, and find a spot to watch the nightly flight of Austin's resident colony of Mexican free-tailed bats.

①

④ Belt it out at EGO'S

Late-night karaoke is a staple in Austin, but nowhere does it better than Ego's. Order a craft beer, select your anthem, and sing your heart out to the good-time crowd.

*Since it opened in 1955, **The Continental Club** has hosted the likes of musical legends Stevie Ray Vaughan and Sonic Youth.*

Settle in at JUNE'S ALL DAY

Sip on an obscure American wine from the monthly menu and nibble Spanish-style tapas at this all-day café. Get here early to nab a seat on the patio.

② ③ Raise a glass at WATERTRADE

Get a taste of contemporary cocktail culture at this stylish lounge, which specializes in Japanese whiskies and sake.

Butler Metro Park

BARTON SPRINGS ROAD

Colorado River

East Bouldin Creek

BOULDIN AVENUE

SOUTH 1ST STREET

East Bouldin Creek

SOUTH CONGRESS AVE

EAST RIVERSIDE DRIVE

BOULDIN CREEK

NEWTON STREET

CONGRESS AVENUE

SOUTH CONGRESS AVENUE

WEST MONROE ST

SOUTH CONGRESS

EAST MONROE ST

WEST ANNIE ST

EAST ANNIE STREET

0 meters 400
0 yards 400

SHOP

Forget strip malls and fast fashion: Austinites prefer to shop indie, scouting for swell vintage finds, celebrating local designers, and stocking up on organic produce.

Thrift and Vintage Stores

Austinites love all things unique, and the city's thrift and vintage stores are a good place to build an original aesthetic. Here, locals scour the racks for brand-new (at least to them) threads, accessories, and homeware.

UNCOMMON OBJECTS

Map 6; 1602 Fortview Road, South Lamar;
///outfit.shirts.twisting; www.uncommonobjects.com

This co-op of 24 antique sellers has been described as "your eccentric uncle's attic on steroids." And we're not going to argue with that. Think taxidermic animals wearing kids' clothes, old-fashioned signs, and cowboy paraphernalia (this is Texas, after all).

AUSTIN PETS ALIVE! THRIFT

Map 4; 5801 Burnet Road, Brentwood; ///fashion.shovels.sprinkle;
www.austinpetsalive.org/shop/thrift

Austinites are famously dog-obsessed. It's no surprise, then, that locals love this thrift store, which channels all its proceeds into no-kill animal shelter Austin Pets Alive! (where stars Kyle Chandler, Justin Theroux,

Check out Facebook for the store's next event. They often feature live music – and dogs, of course. | and Antoni Porowski have adopted pooches). Sure, the secondhand stock keeps things simple, but this place is all about that feel-good glow.

BLACKFEATHER VINTAGE WORKS

Map 3; 979 Springdale Road Suite #98, Govalle;
///blankets.watching.sparkle; www.blackfeathervintageworks.com

Business badass Jess Nieri pioneered East Sixth Street long before it was a hipster hub, setting up a coffee-shop-meets-community-arts-space there in 1998. And she's brought the same creative flair to her Govalle venture. Not content with the one-of-a-kind aspect of vintage clothing, Jess spends her days altering preloved pieces to give them extra personality and pizzazz. Brocaded sweater vest, anyone?

ROOM SERVICE VINTAGE

Map 4; 117 North Loop Boulevard East, North Loop;
///pressing.panic.ambient; www.roomservicevintage.com

Walking into Room Service Vintage feels like visiting your nana's and papa's home – knickknacks and all. Husband-and-wife team Bill and Lori have a penchant for 50s, 60s and 70s furniture, but they also stock clothing, toys, and magazines from other decades that will have you gasping, "Oh, we had one of those when I was a kid."

» Don't leave without checking out Forbidden Fruit across the street. This female-owned, sex-positive shop has been "keeping Austin kinky" since 1981. You wouldn't find this stuff at your grandma's house.

BUFFALO EXCHANGE

Map 4; 2904 Guadalupe Street, The Drag;
///hello.fuel.runners; www.buffaloexchange.com

Conveniently located near campus, this outpost of the national thrift store chain is stocked and shopped by UT students. It has a constant turnover, but you can always count on finding a perfectly scuffed pair of Doc Martens, artfully ripped jeans, and a cool outfit for the next college costume party.

BIG BERTHA'S PARADISE VINTAGE

Map 4; 112 North Loop Boulevard East, North Loop;
///older.bracelet.received; (512) 444-5908

Austin is a jeans-and-a-tee-city, but Big Bertha's flies the flag for high-end, couture fashion. Spoiler alert: there's no Bertha here. Instead, owner Henry Tarin acts as your personal stylist, decking

South Congress is a bustling shopping epicenter, but ignore the hordes and follow in-the-know thrifters to the back side of a stone building facing Milton Street. Here, you'll find the green front of Prototype Vintage. It may have racks upon racks of vintage mens- and womenswear, but Prototype specializes in accessories. Its preloved scarves, belts, shoes, and sunglasses have been worn by artists in music videos and at festivals, so you can count on finding just the thing here.

you out in last season's Dolce and Gabbana dresses, golden snakeskin Chloé platforms, and Dior's iconic saddle bags. If you're on a budget, give Big Bertha's a wide berth.

» Don't leave without checking out the glittering jewelry selection. Heck, why not try on some Holly Golightly-style pearls?

GARMENT MODERN + VINTAGE

Map 5; 701 South Lamar Boulevard, South Lamar;
///shocking.taxi.curiosity; www.shopgarment.com

With its custom-designed wood accents, sleek display cases, and racks of sartorial treasures dating from the 1930s to the early 2000s, this store feels more like a museum than a place to shop. But this is where well-heeled South Austinites go to purge and replenish their wardrobes with 90s-era Chanel clutches, patterned Hermès jackets, and fabulous couture Alexander McQueen gowns.

PASSPORT VINTAGE

Map 5; 2217 South 1st Street A, South First;
///respect.scans.survivor; www.passportvintage.com

Y'all know how hard it is to find the perfect pair of jeans. In 2014, denim-fanatics Maria Oliveira and Ryan Lerma set out to make the quest easier, setting up an Etsy shop specializing in the most backside-flattering vintage jeans by Levi's, Wrangler, and more. It soon garnered national acclaim and turned into this cobalt blue brick-and-mortar store. Not sure about your size? They'll take your measurements to ensure a perfect fit.

Austin Style

*Unique jewelry pieces? Check. Locally designed bags?
You got it. Cowboy boots? Well, this is Texas.
Austinites express their personality through their
style, and shop weird (read: indie) whenever possible.*

HATBOX: A MODERN HABERDASHERY

Map 5; 1205 Kinney Avenue, Zilker; ///bits.blues.hoaxes; www.hatbox.com
News flash: Austinites don't all wear cowboy hats. But those who do
get them from Hatbox. This friendly store doesn't just specialize in
classic cowboy headgear, though; wander in and you'll see towers of

Tucked away between artists'
studios in East Austin, Son of
a Sailor *(www.sonofasailor.co)* is
a haven for handmade jewelry
and home decor. Jessica Tata
and Billy Knopp, the duo who
run this little shop together, have
a passion for good craftsmanship
— all Son of a Sailor products
are designed by the pair and
produced in Austin. Stop by to
browse the unique collection,
which includes chunky statement bracelets, soy candles,
leather wallets, and super-cute
enamel pins.

fancy fedoras, smart flatcaps, and many more stylish creations lining the shelves. If you're looking for something to keep the sun out of your eyes – and there's a lot of sun in Texas – you'll find it here.

HELM BOOTS

Map 2; 1200 East 11th Street #101, Central East Austin;
///followers.loss.luggage; www.helmboots.com

Ask any local and they'll tell you two things: one, a great pair of boots is a staple in Austin, and two, if you want to buy some, get them from Helm. Everything about this beloved store seems sturdy: from the soles of the expertly crafted boots to the company ethos that preferences people, product, and profit, in that order. Oh, and on Fridays the staff offer free boot cleaning plus complimentary drinks. Whiskey on the house? It'd be rude to say no.

» Don't leave without asking about Helm's artist party. Once a month, the store showcases local artists and the public are invited in to check out the work on display.

GOOD COMPANY

Map 1; 918 West 12th Street, Clarksville;
///tornado.smirks.second; www.goodcompany.shop

If easy, breezy, and carefree are attractive adjectives, then Good Company is the store for you. Owner and designer Mallary Carroll's womenswear is known for its playful prints, subtle details, and fine cotton. And it's not just Mallary's designs that you'll find here; Good Company supports and stocks emerging local designers, too.

STAG

**Map 5; 1423 South Congress Avenue, South Congress;
///approve.barks.search; www.stagprovisions.com**

Picture the modern Texan man. He's probably bearded, tattooed, and wearing high-quality denim and heritage workwear. And there's a decent chance he got his outfit (and pomade) from Stag. This store specializes in all-American menswear labels, such as Hamilton and Levi's, and it's the only place in the state that stocks the Ralph Lauren line RRL. Yes, it all sounds very hipster – and that's exactly what it is.

» Don't leave without walking down South Congress to Stag's sister store, Daughters. The womenswear stocked here has a similarly laid-back aesthetic, with denim shirts, high-rise jeans, and baggy overalls.

NINA BERENATO

**Map 6; 3200 Palm Way #152, North Loop;
///official.indirect.pricing; www.ninaberenato.com**

Designer Nina Berenato started out with a mobile jewelry store in a converted trailer in Austin (y'all know how much locals love their trucks). Since then she's become a bit of a celebrity among Austin's maker community, founding her own brick-and-mortar store as well as dressing world-famous musicians – including Alicia Keys and Beyoncé – with her designs. Nina still creates everything in her bright and bold line by hand, which is all made using recycled materials as well as ethically sourced stones. So the jewelry's sustainable, plus it's got the approval of Queen B – who are we to question that?

CONSUELA AUSTIN

Map 4; 3500 Guadalupe Street Suite B, Central Austin;
///cake.space.sitting; www.consuelastyle.com

Consuela is where the fun's at. Head over to this joyful store and you'll be greeted by super-friendly staff; a ceiling of dazzling disco balls; brightly painted tables; and sunny, yellow walls. And we haven't even got to the kaleidoscope of colorful bags yet. Expect vibrant totes with jewel-like tones and eccentric prints, all inspired by Mexican designs.

MIRANDA BENNETT STUDIO

Map 2; 1211 East 11th Street, Central East Austin;
///stubble.dividing.brighter; www.shopmirandabennett.com

Miranda Bennett was shocked when she discovered the environmental impact of the fashion industry as a student. Her studio aims to redress the balance — she's partnered with a local manufacturer that trains up refugees, the clothes are colored with natural dyes, and every fabric scrap is utilized. Goodbye fast fashion.

Try it!
MAKE YOUR OWN JEWELS

Learn to create rings and necklaces at Nina Berenato's welcoming workshop *(www. ninaberenato.com)*. Wine flows freely as groups of friends learn the art of metallurgy and stone placement.

Farmers' Markets and Grocers

Shopping at the local farmers' market or grocer is a weekend tradition for many families and friends here. With a coffee in hand, they browse the farm-fresh produce and pick up ingredients for the week ahead.

MT SUPERMARKET

Map 6; 10901 North Lamar Boulevard, North Lamar;
///live.unto.revision; www.mtsupermarket.com

Looking for fresh lychees? Bamboo shoots? Chicken feet? You'll find them at MT Supermarket, Austin's largest Asian superstore. Here, mock meat made from tempeh, wheat, and soy sits alongside traditional Thai, Chinese, and Vietnamese produce.

WHOLE FOODS

Map 1; 525 North Lamar Boulevard, Downtown; ///groups.indoor.kinder;
www.wholefoodsmarket.com/stores/lamar

Frustrated at the lack of organic produce in Austin's supermarkets, hippie couple John Mackey and Renee Lawson set up Whole Foods in 1980. It had a tough start – located in a 100-year flood zone, the uninsured building was hit by the 1981 Memorial Day flash flood. But the community rallied around the store, cleaning up, making repairs, and lending money, and the flagship soon moved to this watertight location. Now owned by corporate giant Amazon, it might seem like Whole Foods has forgotten its humble beginnings, but this branch retains some of the store's original quirky charm – like a rooftop dining area that turns into an outdoor ice rink each winter.

TEXAS FARMERS' MARKET

Map 3; 2006 Philomena Street, Mueller;
///plunge.enable.handwriting; www.texasfarmersmarket.org

On Sundays, it seems like everyone and anyone can be found at this Texas-size market. Here, they fill their tote bags with veggies, baked goods, and artisan produce (and try to resist the tempting aromas from the food truck park – without much success).

>> **Don't leave without** visiting the Austin Kefir Microbrewery stand for a glass of Mircalo – a nonalcoholic, gluten-free bubbly. Cheers!

SALT & TIME

Map 2; 1912 East 7th Street, Central East Austin;
///shunts.month.drifting; www.saltandtime.com

Texans love their steak – so much so that Texas has the most cattle of any state. But Austinites and Texans are very different beasts, so at Salt & Time, meat is given the capital treatment. This butcher sources from sustainable local ranches and is passionate about using every cut. Heck, you can even learn how to carve up a carcass yourself here.

BARTON CREEK FARMERS MARKET

Map 6; 2901 South Capital of Texas Highway, West Lake Hills;
///tones.leads.exactly; www.bartoncreekfarmersmarket.org

Every Saturday morning, this farmers' market sets up in Barton
Creek Square Mall's parking lot to show the retail center how
shopping should be done. Accompanied by strumming musicians
(take that, mall music), early risers hop between stalls, grazing on
sample produce as they go. Food aside, there's plenty else to buy,
from artisan soaps to fresh flowers to handmade jewelry.

» Don't leave without trying Mum Foods' pastrami. Brined, coated in
coriander and pepper, and smoked for ten hours, it's the best in town.

BOGGY CREEK FARM

Map 3; 3414 Lyons Road, Boggy Creek;
///lucky.prop.prepares; www.boggycreekfarm.com

What could be more farm-fresh than a literal farm? From Wednesday
to Saturday, Boggy Creek Farm sells its just-picked, organic vegetables
to the public. In addition to Boggy's seasonal veggies, stalls stock
produce from neighboring farms, too.

WHEATSVILLE CO-OP

Map 4; 3101 Guadalupe Street, The Drag;
///flukes.slid.tested; www.wheatsville.coop

A natural food store is hardly unique in Austin, so how come
Wheatsville Co-op is so special? This is a place run by the people
for the people. Literally. The co-op's 24,000 owners influence

Hit up Wheatsville on Thursdays for a $5 community dinner at the hot bar. It always has vegan options.

everything from the items stocked on the shelves to the nonprofits that the store supports each year. How's that for community spirit?

ANTONELLI'S CHEESE SHOP

Map 4; 500 Park Boulevard, Hyde Park; ///flushed.speeds.brass; www.antonellischeese.com

In an old, restored house in Hyde Park, Antonelli's has been quietly sating Austinites' cheese cravings for over a decade. In addition to the standard offerings, it stocks all sorts of boutique farm cheeses – from local goats' milk feta to Californian Humboldt Fog. But don't worry if you don't know your cheddar from your caprino; Antonelli's makes up picnic-ready cheese and charcuterie trays that take all the decision-making out of the process.

SFC FARMERS' MARKET DOWNTOWN

Map 1; 422 Guadalupe Street, Downtown; ///enabling.grazes.second; www.sustainablefoodcenter.org

In some cities, new couples prove their mettle by shopping in IKEA. In Austin, you know you're in a long-term relationship when you hit up the SFC Farmers' Market. On Saturday mornings, love's young dreams stroll hand-in-hand along Guadalupe Street, stocking up on sustainable produce for tonight's date night as they go. The most solid of couples might adopt a doggo at one of the pop-up events, but yoga, live music, and seed swaps require less commitment.

Book Nooks

Austin's bookstores cater to everyone: students debate radical reads at book clubs, avid collectors pour over rare editions in-store, and local authors recite their latest fiction to intimate audiences.

BOOKPEOPLE

Map 1; 603 North Lamar Boulevard, Downtown;
///shifting.remember.airless; www.bookpeople.com

Whether you're hunting for a new bestseller or you're eager to discover some local fiction, BookPeople's got you covered. With its seemingly endless stock and enviable calendar of events, this giant bookstore is a haven for literary lovers. Join them lingering in the café discussing their latest recommendations, rocking up to the regular in-store book club, and eagerly lining up for a famous author signing.

FIRST LIGHT BOOK SHOP

Map 4; 4300 Speedway Unit 104, Hyde Park;
///supply.wolf.waving; www.firstlightaustin.com

This mighty good bookstore, set in a former post office, is a beloved local book hub. Inside, the shelves are lined with a curated selection picked by a small group of local book lovers. Expect to be surprised:

the offerings change regularly and cover the likes of cookbooks, bestsellers, and local publications. There's a small café, too, so pull up a chair, grab a bite, and discover a new favorite read.

RESISTENCIA BOOKS
Map 6; 2000 Thrasher Lane, Riverside;
///output.tens.barefoot; www.resistenciabooks.com

World-renowned poet and local activist Raúl R. Salinas founded this bookstore, and its sister organization Red Salmon Arts, in 1983 to promote Latin and Indigenous literature. But it's not just a store. This is a community space, where creatives come for writers' workshops, students attend poetry slams, and the blue dots in this red state join political meetups.

» **Don't leave without** picking up Raúl R. Salinas's prison poetry. While incarcerated, he launched a literature and arts program for inmates and promoted prisoners' rights.

SOUTH CONGRESS BOOKS
Map 4; 3703 Kerbey Lane, Oakmont Heights;
///taxi.includes.affair; www.southcongressbooks.com

Searching for the perfect gift for your book-loving friend? Look no further than this secondhand bookstore. It's a treasure trove of vintage prints, including signed John Steinbeck novels, early edition Tolstoy tomes, and lovingly preserved rare titles. Come the weekend, locals usually flock here to search for presents – even if it's a gift or two for themselves.

MONKEYWRENCH BOOKS

Map 4; 110 North Loop Boulevard East, North Loop;
///succeed.pursuing.owners; www.monkeywrenchbooks.org

Volunteer-run Monkeywrench specializes in nonfiction titles on anarchism, feminism, and race equity. Alongside its diverse literary offerings, this topical bookstore offers a social hub and safe space for its radical regulars, who've made it their second home over the years. Stop by and you might catch a book club or a meetup taking place, where open-minded creatives discuss social issues and political literature. Oh, and keep an eye out for Emma the bookstore cat – she's the unofficial guardian of books here.

BOOKWOMAN

Map 4; 5501 North Lamar Boulevard #A-105, North Lamar;
///crust.jumps.chipper; www.ebookwoman.com

One of the dozen remaining feminist bookstores in the country (and the only one of its kind in Texas), BookWoman has been a local landmark for years. The location may be unremarkable – in a North Lamar strip mall, distinguished by a bright purple awning – but the atmosphere inside is as special as it gets. Cozy and always welcoming, Bookwoman features impeccably curated shelves of female-oriented fiction and nonfiction. Check out the children's section, too, which is well stocked with a number of inclusive works.

>> Don't leave without talking to Susan Post, the store's friendly longtime owner, who once ran the bookstore from her own home. She's full of spot-on recommendations.

Liked by the locals

"Come visit the only feminist bookstore in Texas! BookWoman is full of curated books to educate and inspire every type of reader. We're also celebrating 47 years as a fabulous, intersectional-feminist safe haven for books, gifts, and more."

SUSAN POST, OWNER OF BOOKWOMAN

Home Touches

As much as everybody in Austin would enjoy a center-piece made up of breakfast tacos, society just isn't there yet. In the meantime, pick up some plants, plates, and other home accessories from these cool spots.

SOCO MAKER'S MARKET

Map 5; 1511 South Congress Avenue, South Congress;
///grin.acid.headset; www.socomakersmarket.com

For SoCo residents, there's always time on the weekend for this pop-up market specializing in wares by local artists, makers, and vintage sellers. Live music adds to the buzz as Austinites nudge their way around the stalls, looking to score the next unique addition for their homes, be that a poster, a candle, or a piece of art. The quirkier the find, the better — we are in the capital of weird, after all.

EAST AUSTIN SUCCULENTS

Map 3; 801 Tillery Street, Springdale;
///pages.leopard.heats; www.eastaustinsucculents.com

Locals will tell you it's easy to get lost in this cacti and succulent nursery — it seems to go on forever and house every plant imaginable. This vast array of stock makes it the perfect place for those who keep killing off their houseplants and are in need of a less-vulnerable plant baby (cacti and succulents are as hardy as they come). An added bonus are the super-friendly staff, who'll happily give you advice and customize your plant pots for you. Another bonus: there's a store dog, named Subby, and he's probably one of the cutest pooches around (have a look on the website if you don't believe us).

>> Don't leave without checking out the biggest metal moon cactus in Texas. It makes for a great photo op to commemorate your love of cacti.

THE PAPER + CRAFT PANTRY

Map 3; 1023 Springdale Road, Building 6B, Springdale;
///lovely.code.debating; www.thepapercraftpantry.com

Ready to upgrade that old yellow notepad that you've been scribbling your shopping lists on for as long as you can remember? This cute store is one of our favorite spots in town for stationery, greeting cards, and crafty gifts. It's run by self-confessed stationery-fanatic Pei Sim, who champions products created by small business owners and designers and happily helps you find exactly what you need.

Try it!
GET CRAFTY

Every week The Paper + Craft Pantry hosts a variety of workshops where you can learn skills like block printing and calligraphy — take a look at the calendar online to see what's going on.

BLUE ELEPHANT

Map 4; 4001 North Lamar Boulevard #512, North Lamar;
///shunted.cone.giant; www.shopblueelephant.com

With locally made Barton Springs-scented candles (sea salt and sweet orchid), tote bags (ideal for all those farmers' markets you'll be going to), and logo tees lining the shelves, this inviting boutique is the perfect spot to grab a gift for a friend – or a cute souvenir for yourself. Either way, you're probably not leaving empty-handed.

FROND PLANT SHOP

Map 5; 507-A West Mary Street, Bouldin Creek;
///solution.soft.sobs; www.frondaustin.com

Addicted to houseplants? Us too, and we'll let you in on a little secret: Frond won't cure your cravings. The pots and planters here, usually designed in soft, earthy tones, feel like they were hand-selected from the Instagram grid of an interior design influencer. And the varied plant selection? Just as swoon-worthy. Get your wallet at the ready.

KEITH KREEGER STUDIOS

Map 3; 916 Springdale Road, Building 2-104, Springdale;
///shins.since.recruited; www.keithkreeger.com

Dining out in Austin, there's a good chance you've come across Keith Kreeger's iconic dinnerware, usually in the form of a handcrafted porcelain plate with a signature black stripe across it. And if you happened to really like that plate, there's a more socially acceptable way of getting one than by trying to sneak it into your handbag. In this showroom, you can find Kreeger's cups, plates, vases, and just about everything else you'd need to stylishly decorate your home. Check out the Hand-Thrown section if you want something really one-of-a-kind.

ATOWN
Map 4; 5502 Burnet Road, Allandale;
///deliver.soulful.shape; www.keepatownweird.com

Austin's a great city and the locals know it. If you're feeling just as hyped about this Texan capital as its residents then head to Atown for some Austin-themed creations. From Austinopoly boards games to *The Austin Cookbook* – a veritable bible of local dishes – this store has a whole lotta love for the city. And with the staff there to tell you about the artists you're shopping from, you'll be getting a virtual tour of the local art scene at the same time.

APARTMENT F
Map 2; 1200 East 11th Steet Suite 104, Central East Austin;
///slippers.kipper.install; www.shopaptf.com

Ashley Yetter's carefully curated space is as calm as they come. Soothing scents drift from the apothecary collection as locals peruse the stylish homewares and accessories. The most-prized possessions, however, can be found under your feet: beautiful Moroccan and Persian hand-knotted rugs line the floor of this store, attracting design fans from all over the state.

» Don't leave without asking Ashley how she sources her rugs. She'll be sure to regale you with tales of her adventures.

0 meters   400
0 yards   400

Flick through vinyl at BREAKAWAY RECORDS

Electronica fan? Prefer soul? Whatever music you like, chances are you'll find it in Breakaway's selection of vintage vinyl.

Scour the racks at BIG BERTHA'S PARADISE VINTAGE

Try on a fabulous secondhand outfit at this funky store. Just don't go looking for a bargain – it ain't here.

5

Get inspired at REVIVAL VINTAGE

Looking for a quirky piece to complete your home? Make a beeline for Revival for some interior design inspo.

4

No café reps North Loop's creative vibe better than **Epoch Coffee**, which serves up local art alongside MOJO cold brews.

3 **2**

Browse the shelves at MONKEYWRENCH BOOKS

Bag a book at this volunteer-run, anarchist-leaning store. Check out the events calendar while you're here.

An afternoon shopping in
North Loop

Austinites support their community by shopping small, indie, and local, and nowhere makes that easier than North Loop. Sandwiched between two busy, commercial thoroughfares, this low-slung neighborhood is practically chain-free, lined instead by indie bookshops, vintage stores, and small-batch bakeries. Come the weekend, gaggles of community-minded Austinites flock here, armed with their credit cards and trusty totes.

Fuel up at ZUCCHINI KILL BAKERY

Enjoy a guilt-free treat at this gluten-free, vegan bakery, where classic bakes are given a musical makeover with punk-inspired names.

1. Zucchini Kill Bakery
701 East 53rd Street Suite C, North Loop; www.zucchinikill.com ///thunder.visions.coiling

2. Big Bertha's Paradise Vintage
112 North Loop Boulevard East, North Loop; (512) 444-5908 ///older.bracelet.received

3. Monkeywrench Books
110 North Loop Boulevard East, North Loop; www.monkeywrenchbooks.org ///succeed.pursuing.owners

4. Breakaway Records
211 West North Loop Boulevard, North Loop; www.breakawayrecordshop.com ///vital.leaps.pipeline

5. Revival Vintage
5201 North Lamar Boulevard, North Loop; www.revivalvintageatx.com ///report.fury.watched

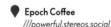 **Epoch Coffee**
///powerful.stereos.social

ARTS & CULTURE

The Texan capital city swells with culture and creativity. And in classic Austin style, the mainstream and the weird and wacky get equal coverage.

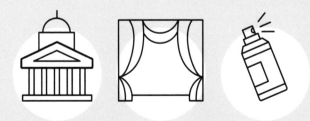

City History

Why is Austin called the Live Music Capital of the World? How come locals are obsessed with Tex-Mex? Find the answers – and so much more – at these history-filled spots.

TEXAS MUSIC MUSEUM

Map 2; 1009 East 11th Street, Central East Austin;
///inferior.trifle.audible; www.texasmusicmuseum.org

We hate to sound like a broken record, but Austin really is the "Live Music Capital of the World," with more music venues per capita than any other US city. The Texas Music Museum is a small nonprofit that explores the history of the city's musical heritage. Its temporary exhibitions cover topics such as the origins

Try it!
WALKING TOUR

So you've heard all about Willie Nelson and SXSW, but what about the Cosmic Cowboy? Discover Austin's offbeat musical history with Austin Music Heritage Tours *(www.austinmusicheritagetours.com).*

of Mexican American conjunto music and the effect of East Austin's gospel churches on blues music, while regular talks are held by local rock, country, and blues musicians.

TEXAS AFRICAN AMERICAN HISTORY MEMORIAL

Map 1; 10 West 11th Street, Downtown; ///approve.bind.graphics

As with any city, Austin's history is full of ups and downs, rights and wrongs. And the city acknowledges its checkered past. In 2016, the Texas African American History Memorial was erected on the grounds of the Texas State Capitol, beside seven monuments to Confederate soldiers. Sculpted by Ed Dwight (who was famously rejected by NASA for being Black), this giant, bronze memorial remembers Juneteenth, the day slavery was abolished in Texas.

UNIVERSITY OF TEXAS TOWER

Map 4; 110 Inner Campus Drive; Campus; ///captive.remit.speaks; www.tower.utexas.edu

You can't talk about Austin without mentioning the University of Texas, whose campus takes up much of the city. Fun fact: Austinites are such devoted Texas Longhorn fans that, unlike other universities, the football program funds academic studies. Whether you're a new student or just curious, you should check out the University of Texas Tower and its library for a taste of this institution's history.

» **Don't leave without** joining a guided tour of the tower. At the top, your aching legs will be rewarded with great views of campus.

BULLOCK STATE HISTORY MUSEUM

Map 4; 1800 Congress Avenue, Downtown; ///dogs.urge.album;
www.thestoryoftexas.com

This Texas-size museum explores the people and events that have shaped the state. The permanent collection is pretty exhaustive, covering everything from Texas's Indigenous communities to the so-bad-they're-good B-movies set in the state.

AUSTIN CENTRAL LIBRARY

Map 1; 710 West Cesar Chavez Street, Downtown;
///beeline.employ.tall; www.library.austintexas.gov

Move over Silicon Valley – tech giants have relocated to cheaper Texas and earned Austin the nickname Silicon Hills. Weirdly, the best place to get familiar with the city's new residents (Bumble and IBM among them) is in the bookish surrounds of this library. At its "technology petting zoo," you can try out everything from 3D printers to smart musical instruments.

EMMA S. BARRIENTOS MEXICAN AMERICAN CULTURAL CENTER

Map 1; 600 River Street, Rainey; ///emails.volcano.costumes;
(512) 974-3772

Did you know that Texas was once part of Mexico? Despite Austin's love of tacos, the city's Mexican heritage has often been sidelined. But this cultural center is working to change that by supporting and exploring the Mexican American experience.

Liked by the locals

"When you think of Austin, you may think tacos, live music, and being outdoors. But I invite you to delve even deeper into Austin's history and discover that Austin's Latin American community is central to this city's identity."

OLIVIA TAMZARIAN, EMMA S. BARRIENTOS MEXICAN AMERICAN CULTURAL CENTER SUPERVISOR

Top Theaters

From century-old performance venues to arthouse cinemas, you'll find a slew of great theaters here. And remember, locals wear boots and sure as heck don't change out of their jeans to go to a show.

BASS CONCERT HALL

Map 4; 2350 Robert Dedman Drive, Campus;
///uses.briefer.matter; www.texasperformingarts.org

You're just as likely to see famous classical ensembles and special symphony performances at this campus concert hall as you are major rock and pop names. The crowd here's just as versatile – depending on the performer you could be surrounded by students, groups of friends seeking some culture, or older folks out on date night.

AFS CINEMA

Map 4; 6259 Middle Fiskville Road, St Johns;
///snipe.dweller.media; www.austinfilm.org

Fan of *Dazed and Confused*? How about *Boyhood*? *School of Rock* anyone? If so, you're in the right place. Local filmmaking legend Richard Linklater founded the Austin Film Society and its partner theater, AFS, here. The beloved theater is the nexus of Austin's indie film culture and

For the budding film-makers out there, Austin Film Society offers regular film workshops and classes. | has suitably cool showings – think edgy documentaries and celebrated foreign films. In the lobby, film fans can peruse Linklater's collection of old movie posters.

ZACH THEATRE

Map 5; 202 South Lamar Boulevard, Zilker;
///march.symphony.ropes; www.zachtheatre.org

Austin's oldest continuously operating theater, the ZACH is perhaps best known for its kid-friendly programing. But if you're not up for seeing *The Sound of Music* for the third or fourth time, don't fear; this intimate and homey theater puts on all kinds of productions. Itching to see contemporary American classics like *Once*, *Hedwig and the Angry Inch*, and *In the Heights*? Keep an eye on this venue's eclectic calendar.

» Don't leave without heading to the ZACH's Serra Skyline Lounge for happy hour and skyline views before the show.

GROUND FLOOR THEATRE

Map 3; 979 Springdale Road #122, Springdale;
///skin.rely.slide; www.groundfloortheatre.org

Nestled between a brewery and a cidery (ideal for predrinks, just saying), this indie theater produces new works by and for under-represented communities. Past productions include two-woman plays, cabarets celebrating Black musical theater, and storytelling projects solely featuring trans and nonbinary community members.

VIOLET CROWN CINEMA

Map 1; 434 West 2nd Street, Downtown;

///gurgled.gateway.dwelled; www.austin.violetcrown.com

Whether you're a sucker for the newest blockbuster or an indie film aficionado, this locally owned theater has you covered. Once the movie's over, enjoy a post-film discussion and drinks on the cinema's leafy terrace – it's perfect for people-watching.

PARAMOUNT THEATRE

Map 1; 713 Congress Avenue, Downtown;

///indoor.mystery.rope; www.austintheatre.org

You won't walk past the Paramount without stopping to admire its ornate exterior – a Classical Revival facade with a huge, glowing sign over the entrance. Austin's century-old theater was once the home of the legendary Sam Houston's War Department of the

Shh!

What was once a sex toy factory in East Austin is now The Museum of Human Achievement *(www.themuseum ofhumanachievement.com)* – a multidisciplinary arts space that hosts a variety of offbeat film screenings, immersive installations, live theater productions, and more. But that's about all we can tell you. Visitors have to become a member of MoHa to get the address and the calendar of events. Are you getting cult vibes yet? Because you should be.

Republic of Texas. The alumni is just as legendary: ever heard of the Marx Brothers or Houdini? Today, this historic (and rumored haunted) venue hosts a variety of acts – from 70mm movie showings to sold-out Sheryl Crow concerts.

BLUE STARLITE DRIVE-IN

Map 3; 500 VFW Roard, North Central;
///freshen.trees.passion; www.bluestarlitedrivein.com

Austin's quirky drive-in makes for the perfect date or evening activity with your gang. Featuring a mix of arthouse films, new releases, and Gen X and Y childhood classics, the venue has seven screens – some for a small number of cars and others for walk-ins. You have the option of adding vintage-style sweet concessions (like Runts and Whoppers, buttery popcorn, and old-fashioned sodas) to your order when you buy tickets, too. It doesn't get more old-school than this.

» Don't leave without seeing a horror flick on the "Forest Screen," a spooky screen tucked away in a dark grove of trees on the property.

HYDE PARK THEATRE

Map 4; 511 West 43rd Street, Hyde Park;
///bagels.smug.twitchy; www.hydeparktheatre.org

You'll get a real sense of Austin's theater community at this itty-bitty spot. Artistic director Ken Webster greets guests warmly at the door (unless he's acting in the performance), and shows usually feature a load of local actors – with their enthusiastic friends filling up the audience. P.S. There are only 50 seats, so book your tickets in advance.

Art Galleries

Art galleries in Austin run the gamut from the highbrow to the gritty to the just plain weird. And it's not just the big-hitter venues that dictate the scene – indie galleries in this city punch far above their weight.

WALLY WORKMAN GALLERY

Map 1; 1202 West 6th Street, Clarksville;
///colder.code.punk; www.wallyworkmangallery.com

Tired of the classics and want to see something new? Head to this 100-year-old house, which is a haven for emerging artists. Sure, the floorboards are a little worn, but the art on display is as fresh as it gets. Think vibrant, contemporary pieces – the sort art students and expert collectors can't help but pause in front of to discuss.

GRAYDUCK GALLERY

Map 2; 2213 East Cesar Chavez Street, Holly;
///treating.divisions.flushed; www.grayduckgallery.com

Housed in one of Austin's ubiquitous bungalows is local favorite grayDUCK Gallery. Monthly exhibits here focus on a particular artist's work, which can range from playful photography series to kaleidoscopic paintings adorning the whitewashed walls. The gallery also serves as a hub for Austin's creatives, frequently hosting poetry readings, indie film screenings, live music, and a variety of other events.

» Don't leave without sitting on the leafy patio at Counter Culture, just a few doors down, with a spiced chai kombucha (because, hey, if you're already having an East Side art-hipster moment, why not embrace it?).

AUSTIN ART GARAGE
Map 5; 2200 South Lamar Boulevard, Galindo;
///trailers.reminds.goggles; www.austinartgarage.com

Austin is an arty capital, and nowhere showcases the range of creativity in these parts better than the Austin Art Garage. It's a hub of contemporary local art, most of which is available to purchase, but if you're not in the market for new wall art, you can simply appreciate the ever-changing displays on the walls. And who knows? You might just be persuaded to invest in a modern Texan masterpiece.

WOMEN & THEIR WORK
Map 2; 1311 East Cesar Chavez Street, East Cesar Chavez;
///mirror.trip.inhaled; www.womenandtheirwork.org

You can probably guess what the focus is here. For over 40 years, this gallery has been a valuable part of Austin's feminist art scene, featuring lauded contemporary works by women. Expect thought-provoking work – from absorbing installations to striking paintings – in a friendly and inclusive space. Oh, and admission is free. We'll see you there.

Solo, Pair, Crowd

Creativity in Austin knows no bounds. Whether indoors or out, there's art to suit every taste in this city.

FLYING SOLO

Art walk for one

Nature meets art in Laguna Gloria — part outdoor sculpture gallery and part meditation garden. Take a turn yourself and admire the life-size pieces set against a backdrop of glistening water and not-so-meditative peacock calls.

IN A PAIR

Culture for a couple

Wondering where to go for an arty date? Head to La Peña. Specializing in Latino art, this intimate gallery is the perfect place for a cultural tête-à-tête.

FOR A CROWD

A friendly debate

Gather the gang and take a stroll around the Contemporary Austin — Jones Center. You'll need a good discussion with friends to fully appreciate the modern art on display here.

MEXIC-ARTE MUSEUM

Map 1; 419 Congress Avenue, Downtown;
///reef.probably.dent; www.mexic-artemuseum.org

From the murals covering the exterior to the multidisciplinary work inside, contemporary Mexican art comes in all forms at this favorite museum. To top it all off, every spring, the Mexic-Arte sponsors the Taste of Mexico festival (where you can explore the diversity of Mexican cuisine through dozens of food samples). Don't miss it.

LORA REYNOLDS GALLERY

Map 1; The 360 Tower, Downtown;
///removed.gravest.bouncing; www.lorareynolds.com

A heavyweight on the local arts scene, this high-end gallery shows work by emerging, midcareer, and established artists in a wide variety of media. It's located in a ritzy part of Downtown, so expect a classy crowd of young professionals and art critics to match.
» Don't leave without strolling through nearby Republic Square and fueling up on gourmet snacks and drinks at Salt & Time Cafe.

BLANTON MUSEUM OF ART

Map 4; 200 East Martin Luther King Jr Boulevard, Campus;
///shadow.sleeping.posts; www.blantonmuseum.org

UT's Blanton is where students come to get their art fix – whether they're sketching the work on display or discussing the latest exhibit. When uni life gets hectic, you'll find them wandering around Ellsworth Kelly's serene churchlike structure outside (the late artist's final project).

Favorite Museums

Think of a museum and a dusty, musty institution may come to mind. Not so in Austin. Here, a trash heap has been turned into art and an animatronic Lyndon B. Johnson talks you through history.

HARRY RANSOM CENTER

**Map 4; 300 West 21st Street, Campus; ///vanilla.goods.treble;
www.hrc.utexas.edu**

Bookworms, we got you. The Harry Ransom Center on the south end of the UT campus is home to a huge collection of rare books and literary documents. And, seeing as it doesn't cost a dollar (a novelty when it comes to Austin's museums), folks flock here on the regular to check out Jack Kerouac's writing journals, Edgar Allen Poe's writing desk, and a copy of the Gutenburg Bible.

NEILL-COCHRAN HOUSE MUSEUM

**Map 4; 2310 San Gabriel, West Campus; ///balanced.highs.export;
www.nchmuseum.org**

Where other institutions built by enslaved people have stayed very quiet, the Neill-Cochran House Museum actively engages with its problematic origins. And up-front Austinites love this museum for it,

For scavenger hunts and lawn games, check social media for the museum's next Sunday Funday Event. | coming here frequently to learn about the city's 19th-century history. The events are also big draws: book clubs, family-fun days, and the odd yoga class.

THE THINKERY

Map 3; 1830 Simond Avenue, Mueller;
///forgets.mistress.curbed; www.thinkeryaustin.org

For most of the month, this hands-on science museum is bursting with sticky swarms of kids. But on Thinkery21 nights, it's the grown-ups' turn to play. On one Thursday each month, pop-up trucks start serving drinks and snacks, DJs spin some funky tunes, and adults-only talks and hands-on activities explore a theme – such as "Forces of Nature," which featured "Carbon Footprint Monopoly" and "Super (Farmers') Market Sweep."

» Don't leave without asking about the next Two Scientists Walk into a Bar event, when you can grill a couple of scientists about the intricacies of life over a drink at their neighborhood bar.

MUSEUM OF THE WEIRD

Map 1; 412 East 6th Street, Red River Cultural District;
///grape.banks.painters; www.museumoftheweird.com

This place is more of a cabinet of curiosities than a museum. Playing up to Austin's "weird" reputation, the Museum of the Weird is full of shrunken heads, circus memorabilia, and malformed mammals, such as a "cyclops pig." It's definitely not for everyone.

CATHEDRAL OF JUNK

Map 6; 4422 Lareina Drive, South Austin;
///paint.slippers.legend; (512) 299-7413

You've heard the phrase "one man's trash is another man's treasure," and now's your chance to judge whether it's true. Using everything from baubles to bike parts, artist Vince Hannemann has created his very own Notre-Dame out of garbage – complete with vaulted passageways and a throne room. And despite some red-blooded residents demanding its removal, city officials have stood by Vince's backyard project since he started it in 1989. (The city only asked Vince to remove broken electronics from the structure, whereupon he promptly set up the Zen Garden of TVs.) It's creative, sustainable, and, dare we say it, a little bit weird. Give Vince a call to set up a visit (note: he doesn't always check his voicemails).

» Don't leave without giving a $10 donation. Vince funds the cathedral and his other art projects through showing people around.

GEORGE WASHINGTON CARVER MUSEUM

Map 2; 1165 Angelina Street, Central East Austin;
///revision.protests.call; www.austintexas.gov/department/george-washington-carver-museum-cultural-and-genealogy-center

This East Austin institution is more than a museum; it's a hub for African American culture. With four art galleries, a 134-seat theater, a dance studio, and a darkroom on top of the permanent exhibition on African American history, the museum shines an important spotlight on a group who are often underrepresented or ignored in mainstream museums. Add free admission, lectures, and workshops on everything from creative writing to hip-hop dancing, and it's no wonder that Austinites keep coming back for more.

LBJ PRESIDENTIAL LIBRARY

Map 4; 2313 Red River Street, Campus;
///liners.pages.glosses; www.lbjlibrary.org

This library-meets-museum is dedicated to Austin's most famous resident. Actor Matthew McConaughey? Yoga YouTuber Adriene Mishler? More like 36th president Lyndon B. Johnson. Swerve the life-size animatronic LBJ, which is almost as creepy as it is informative, and check out one of the rotating exhibitions instead. Whether it's on Motown or minorities in sports, you can bet that it'll be worth that encounter with the robotic Democrat.

THE COLOR INSIDE

Map 4; 2201 Speedway, Campus; ///object.bikes.dealings;
www.turrell.utexas.edu

Where do artsy Austinites go for provocative art that's made in the US? It may have more of a reputation for books and football fans, but the University of Texas is also home to the Landmarks public art program. Its crowning glory is James Turrell's "skyspace" *The Color Inside.* Here, visitors sit (or lie) in a large room, which has a large circular hole in its ceiling. Over the course of time – minutes, hours, or until their patience wears thin – they watch the changing colors of the sky. You'll have to be quick to nab a sunset ticket.

Street Art

Many of Austin's murals act as historical records or political statements. But that doesn't mean that they're not fun. This city has an excellent sense of humor and isn't afraid to poke fun at itself.

GREETINGS FROM AUSTIN

Map 5; 1720 South 1st Street; South First; ///without.inserted.forecast

Plastered on postcards, guidebooks, and just about every Austinite's social media feed, the *Greetings From Austin* mural could seem a bit, well, yawn. But we couldn't not include it. Fashioned on a 50s postcard, complete with Austin landmarks, it's where new residents go to proclaim their allegiance to the city – on Instagram, at least.

» Don't leave without grabbing a gelato from Dolce Neve across the street. An ice-cream cone will complete your vintage-style snap.

WE RISE

Map 2; 1902 East 12th Street, East 12th District; ///escape.buzzing.flesh

This mural's title couldn't be more appropriate. In 2014, artist Chris Rogers painted a dozen Black American icons on this large wall in a tribute to East Austin's rich heritage. Three years later, he awoke to hundreds of outraged texts and tweets telling him that his mural had been painted over by a new art gallery. With the neighborhood's historically Black population dwindling as a result of rising rents, the destruction of the mural became a symbol of the area's gentrification and whitewashing. (Despite the fact that Las Cruxes, the gallery responsible for the mural's destruction, promotes Mexican American culture.) City leaders responded to local feeling by commissioning Rogers to recreate his work, and the rebooted *We Rise* depicts even more Black icons than the original.

YOU'RE MY BUTTER HALF

Map 3; 2000 East Martin Luther King Jr Boulevard, Chestnut; ///editor.lays.ocean

Of course, this Austin love story features food. This super-sweet mural depicts a piece of toast and slab of butter proclaiming their feelings. It's simple, but very effective, and cuddled-up couples flock here to use it as a backdrop for their social media posts — especially if they've just got engaged. Steadfastly single? Don't be put off; this mural will steal your heart, no matter your relationship status.

Try it!
PAINT YOUR OWN

Indulge your inner artist at the Hope Outdoor Gallery, near the airport. Pick up some spray paint from the on-site store and set to work making your own mural (*www.hopeoutdoorgallery.com*).

TAU CETI

Map 1; 201 East 2nd Street, Downtown; ///miracle.unwell.decorate

You can't miss this one. Literally. At 103 ft (31 m) and painted in every shade of the rainbow, it's the city's tallest and most eye-catching mural. Artist Josef Kristofoletti claims that his work represents the unity and diversity of the city, because the varied hues in the visible light spectrum appear one color to the human eye. Deep, right?

HI, HOW ARE YOU

Map 4; 408 West 21st Street, Campus; ///vitals.remarks.fast

It may not be much to look at, but this scrawled line drawing is an important piece of Austin's musical heritage. This froglike creature – or Jeremiah, The Innocent as it's officially called – was painted by musician Daniel Johnston in 1993 to celebrate the release of his *Hi, How Are You* album. Who? Johnston never hit the big time, handing out his cassettes to customers while working at Austin's McDonald's,

Shh!

Just two blocks down from *Hi, How Are You* – on West 23rd Street – you'll find a mural that dates back to 1974. Local artists Kerry Awn, Tommy Bauman, and Rick Turner created *Austintacious* at the height of Austin's hippie phase. With city founder Stephen F. Austin at its center, the mural pokes fun at classic Austin scenes. It's been tagged many times over the years, but the community always rallies together to restore it.

but his lo-fi music influenced the likes of Flaming Lips and Nirvana. Heck, Kurt Cobain was even spotted wearing a Jeremiah T-shirt. Stop by the mural to show Johnston the appreciation he deserves.

WILLIE FOR PRESIDENT
Map 5; 1423 South Congress Avenue, South Congress; ///approve.barks.search

Now here's an Austinite everyone loves. There are countless spray-painted depictions of country music star Willie Nelson in this city, but this one on the side of hipster menswear store Stag is the most glorifying. In the year that Donald Trump won the election, and Texas voted overwhelmingly red, Austin decided that Willie would make a better president than any other candidate. We're inclined to agree.

I LOVE YOU SO MUCH
Map 5; 1300 South Congress Avenue, South Congress; ///interval.promotes.tested

Who loves who so much? Is it the remnants of a proposal? A love letter to the city? Not many Austinites know the cute story behind the pink letters on the green wall of Jo's Coffee. Musician Amy Cook sprayed this simple declaration on the side of her girlfriend Liz Lambert's café in 2010. Since then, countless folk have reclaimed this mural's timeless sentiment as their own.

» Don't leave without grabbing an iced turbo from Jo's Coffee. This icy chocolate, hazelnut, coffee, and cream drink is sure to cool you down on a sweltering Texan day.

Chow down at SAM'S BBQ

Test out Sam's claim that "You don't need no teeth to eat my beef" under the hopeful (or hungry) eyes of the Dr. Martin Luther King Jr. mural.

Listen and learn at the AFRICAN AMERICAN CULTURAL AND HERITAGE FACILITY

What was once the home of Thomas Dedrick, a prominent member of Austin's African American community in the late 19th century, is now an African American cultural center. Learn about Black Austin at one of the talks.

CENTRAL EAST AUSTIN

Discover Black history at the GEORGE WASHINGTON CARVER MUSEUM

Housed in what used to be a segregated library, George Washington Carver Museum is dedicated to telling the stories of Austin's Black American community. Scope out the exhibitions or join a workshop.

Catch a performance in KENNY DORHAM'S BACKYARD

Named after a groundbreaking Black jazz trumpeter, this outdoor venue hosts a variety of musicians. Check out the events calendar before joining a crowd of like-minded fans.

Fuel up at ANYTHING'S BAKED POTATO

At this restaurant, anything goes – on a baked potato, that is. Choose from the likes of Cajun shrimp, fried chicken, and sautéed salmon.

A historically Black college, **Huston-Tillotson University** *became the city's first institution of higher learning when it opened in 1875.*

Once a segregated space only for Black Americans, **Rosewood Park** is now a green space for everyone and hosts regular festivals.

CHESTNUT

PLEASANT VALLEY RD

AVENUE

Boggy Creek

EAST AUSTIN

AST 7TH STREET

A day exploring
Six Square

As part of the now-infamous 1928 city plan, Black Americans were relocated to "Six Square" – the six square miles east of what is now the I-35. Today, the name has been reclaimed by the Black artists and entrepreneurs who have lived in this area for generations and are proud to call it home. Here, cooks barbecue on pits their grandparents once used, artists create politically motivated works, and craftspeople continue the family trade.

1. African American Cultural and Heritage Facility
912 East 11th Street, Central East Austin; (512) 974-2424
///repaid.highways.monitors

2. Anything's Baked Potato
1326 Rosewood Avenue, Central East Austin;
www.anythingsaustin.com
///chained.locator.post

3. George Washington Carver Museum
1165 Angelina Street, Central East Austin;
(512) 974-4926
///reddish.improves.rejects

4. Sam's BBQ
2000 East 12th Street, 12th Street Cultural District;
(512) 478-0378
///rollers.fault.podcast

5. Kenny Dorham's Backyard
1106 East 11th Street, Central East Austin; (512) 538-5657
///approve.festivity.sticky

📍 **Huston-Tillotson University**
///wire.examiner.defeat

📍 **Rosewood Park**
///herring.manhole.minerals

NIGHTLIFE

Nights out in this city are easygoing and downright fun. Friends turn competitors on game nights, groups two-step at honky-tonks, and musicians play in intimate venues.

Honky-Tonkin'

Honky-tonks are hard to pin down; the term applies to both neighborhood bars and two-stepping dance halls. The common denominator? Country music. So grab a drink and a partner, and hit the dance floor.

BROKEN SPOKE

Map 6; 3201 South Lamar Boulevard, South Lamar; ///leaps.jelly.climbing; www.brokenspokeaustintx.net

What do Willie Nelson, the Dixie Chicks, Garth Brooks, and Ray Benson have in common? They've all played at the Broken Spoke. This legendary venue has supported local and big-name musicians since its founding in the 60s. And it's overcome many obstacles in its storied history: the rapid development of surrounding South Lamar,

Try it!
LEARN TO TWO-STEP

New to two-stepping, or just feeling a bit rusty? From 8pm on Fridays and Saturdays, Broken Spoke runs free dance lessons. As well as the two-step, you'll master some western swing and Cotton-eyed Joe moves.

robberies, and the death of owner and honky-tonk hero James White in 2021. A city treasure, we're betting on Austinites two-stepping at this institution for many years to come.

WHITE HORSE
Map 2; 500 Comal Street, Central East Austin; ///handle.fruit.central; www.thewhitehorseaustin.com

The lovely thing about Austin's honky-tonks is that they're multi-generational. And nowhere is this more apparent than at White Horse, where gray-haired couples show off their moves to tripping millennials with two left feet. The old guard love it for the nightly live bluegrass, country, and Americana tunes, while hipsters fawn over its kitsch photo booth, pool tables, and wall of draft whiskeys.

» **Don't leave without** ordering a "Texas Two Step" (a shot of whiskey and a Lone Star beer) – it's sure to loosen up your limbs.

SAM'S TOWN POINT
Map 6; 2115 Allred Drive, South Austin; ///pool.recycled.mediators; www.samstownpointatx.com

Austinites are always reminiscing about the city's heyday – though they can't seem to agree when it was. Why not settle on 1979, when Sam's Town Point first opened? This no-frills honky-tonk has little changed since; there are no craft cocktails in sight and the burgers are served on value-brand buns. What's new is the young crowd of regulars, who trek out to this bar – which once straddled the border with Travis County – to get a taste of the real "Austin City Limits."

LITTLE LONGHORN SALOON

Map 4; 5434 Burnet Road, Allandale; ///tiny.flamed.droplet;
www.thelittlelonghornsaloon.com

It may be known for its Sunday chickens*** bingo but, for the other six nights of the week, Little Longhorn Saloon hosts some of Austin's coolest honky-tonk acts. Like Ameripolitan singer Dale Watson, whose tunes are a mash-up of the honky-tonk, swing, rockabilly, and outlaw genres.

DONN'S DEPOT

Map 4; 1600 West 5th Street, Clarksville; ///woven.deck.physical;
(512) 478-0336

What could be cooler than a honky-tonk set in an old train depot, complete with railcars-turned-restrooms? We'll wait. While you're thinking, order a beer, pull up a chair, and enjoy the sound of owner Donn Adelman tinkling the keys and crooning a country ballad.

» Don't leave without swinging by nearby Tex-Mex restaurant El Arroyo to check out its sign out front. Expect slogans such as "my soulmate is out there somewhere, pushing a pull door."

GIDDY UPS

Map 6; 12010 Menchaca Road, Menchaca; ///propping.toasting.vampire;
www.giddyups.com

People don't really come to Giddy Ups to dance. Instead, the trucker-hat-clad crowd gather to play shuffleboard and board games, while listening to up-and-coming country artists. If you like what you hear, stick some bills in the very Texas tip jar.

Liked by the locals

"Well, honky-tonks used to be our nightclubs here in Austin – they were beer-drinking dance halls. If you wanted liquor, you had to brown-bag it. But it's a different flavor nowadays."

DONN ADELMAN, OWNER OF
DONN'S DEPOT

Cool Clubs

Don't expect a high-gloss nightclub scene (Dallas, this ain't). In keeping with the city's ethos, Austin's clubs tend toward the laid-back and mildly eccentric. But don't fret – there's still plenty of dancing to be had.

BARBARELLA

Map 1; 611 Red River Street, Red River Cultural District; ///sides.airports.busters; (512) 476-7716

Don't get your days mixed up at this Red River staple; each one has a different theme. Madonna and Gaga dominate on Tuezgayz, emo tunes are played on Jimmy Eat Wednesdays, and rock 'n' roll blares out on Grits 'n' Gravy Thursdays. But whenever you rock up to Barbs, you can count on cheap drinks, no judgment, and great music (if you love the classics, that is).

THE VOLSTEAD LOUNGE

Map 2; 1500 East 6th Street; Central East Austin; ///chapels.fake.spilling; www.texashotelvegas.com

Every Venn diagram has a center and that's exactly where you'll find Volstead Lounge. It's kinda like a gritty dive bar cosplaying as a cool nightclub, and it's kept the best bits of both: the city's hottest

Volstead shares its patio with neighboring bar, Hotel Vegas, so you can hop between the two with ease.

DJs and occasional live music acts, New Orleans-style cocktails and tallboy beers, an intimate interior and a huge, no-frills patio. What's not to like?

SAHARA LOUNGE

Map 3; 1413 Webberville Road, Springdale; ///premiums.welfare.slows; www.saharalounge.com

We can't think of a club that sums up Austin's MO better. First, Sahara is run by a mother-and-son team. Second, said owners are musicians: Eileen Bristol plays electric bass and performs with the Africa Night house band, while her son Topaz McGarrigle seems to have mastered every musical instrument you can think of. And, finally, it's got that laid-back vibe that has long-time locals exclaiming it's "the way Austin used to be."

>> Don't leave without trying one of Sahara's signature shots. The Akpateshi is made with rum and African herbs, while the spicy Devil's Piss is a shot of vodka infused with five different hot peppers.

SUMMIT

Map 1; 120 West 5th Street, Warehouse District; ///snails.mornings.koala; www.summitaustin.com

Want to kick off the weekend in style? This swanky rooftop bar, nestled between Downtown's skyscrapers, is the only place to be on Friday nights. Here, the afterwork crowd groove to EDM, wave sparklers, pop champagne, and forget about the weekly grind.

RIO

Map 1; 601 Rio Grande Street, Downtown; ///curable.barman.wardrobe; (512) 436-8464

If you're after a low-key bar to hang with friends and catch up over a beer, look again. Rio is all about the ritzier things in life. Think bottle service, a rooftop pool, and three floors of DJs playing the latest dance anthems. If that sounds like your dream Saturday night, then dress to impress (there's a dress code, obviously) and get in line — this place tends to draw a crowd.

COCONUT CLUB

Map 1; 310B Colorado Street, Downtown; ///snitch.running.duration; (512) 900-6577

This tropical-themed club is one of the hottest places in Austin. Literally. Its owners, Cheer Up Charlies (p157) vets Cole Evans and Brian Almaraz, set out to create an old-fashioned, loud, sweaty nightclub,

Shh!

Flamingo Cantina (www.flamingocantina.com) may sit squarely on Dirty Sixth Street, but it feels a world away from the bro-y fray this district is known for. In this intimate club, the laid-back crowd bops to music that you're unlikely to hear in any other club: Rastafarian reggae, ska, Afro-Cuban jazz, worldbeat, and more. Flamingo Cantina calls it "good vibes music" — and we couldn't agree more.

and, boy, did they succeed. The strobe-lit and pink-hued dance floor is always pulsating with perspiring partygoers. When you need to cool down and catch your breath, retreat to the rooftop lounge and order a frozen drink (a piña colada is the obvious choice). Hello, second wind.

» Don't leave without sating the late-night munchies with a vegan eggplant chorizo arepa from Cuatro Gato, the club's café.

THE ROSE ROOM

Map 6; 11500 East Rock Rose Avenue, North Burnet;
///dazzling.sheet.humidity; www.theroseroom.club

Fancy a night out Vegas-style? You better head to The Rose Room – it's probably the closest Austin gets to a "super club." Inside, revelers are greeted by a glowing pink escalator, six bars on the first floor alone, and two further floors of flashing floor-to-ceiling LED lights. Add the pumping EDM tracks, roving performers, and the flirting and twerking crowd, and you're in for a big night. So much for laid-back.

ELYSIUM

Map 1; 705 Red River Street, Red River Cultural District;
///cheesy.riding.both; www.elysiumonline.net

Located in an old warehouse, and marked by an unassuming sign, this Austin institution has been quietly championing alternative music since 2001. And although the building itself could do with some TLC, the club really is a haven for fans of anything that flies under the radar. Think synth-pop, new wave, post punk, goth, industrial, indie dance, K-pop, and everything in between.

Live Music

Austin is the Live Music Capital of the World. Find out why by checking out the city's theaters, clubs, and bars. You'll have plenty to choose from – Austin has more live music venues per capita than any other city.

ANTONE'S

Map 1; 305 East 5th Street, Downtown; ///abode.outlines.bother; www.antonesnightclub.com

If you're on the hunt for a slice of the city's music history, head to this iconic nightclub. It's been repping blues music since 1975 and has a knack for hosting the most decade-defining acts (Muddy Waters, Jimmy Reed, and Stevie Ray Vaughan are among its alumni). Rising rents have forced Antone's to relocate several times in the past, but it's now back in bluesy Downtown.

STUBB'S BBQ

Map 1; 801 Red River Street, Red River Cultural District; ///speaking.fairway.strongly; www.stubbsaustin.com

Now here's a Southern story. Christopher B. Stubblefield – or "Stubb" – learned how to smoke brisket from his parents. After serving with the last all-Black army infantry in the Korean War, he opened his first restaurant, filled the juke with blues, and unwittingly created a musical hot spot. Legends such as Willie Nelson and Johnny Cash sang for their supper here. And today? Everyone from DJs to folk singers plays Stubb's outdoor ampitheater.

» Don't leave without booking a ticket for the next Gospel Brunch. The rousing music and BBQ meats will fuel both body and soul.

THE MOODY THEATER

Map 1; 310 West Willie Nelson Boulevard, 2nd Street District;
///hounded.purist.holds; www.acl-live.com

The Moody Theater is best known for hosting the acclaimed PBS series and longest-running music show in TV history, *Austin City Limits*. In addition to tapings, this huge venue hosts around 100 other concerts a year. Expect well-known indie acts like Beach House and Fleet Foxes, as well as some hometown heroes such as Gary Clark Jr.

For a musical experience that flies firmly under the radar, check out the Electric Church *(5018 East Cesar Chavez Street)*. Members of the psychedelic rock group Sun Machine and visual artist Fez Moreno took over this abandoned church and turned it into an exciting underground performance space, where rollicking psych and punk bands perform until the early hours. You'll have to check social media for more info – maybe... gigs aren't all that well advertised.

Solo, Pair, Crowd

Whether you're looking for a quiet, relaxing evening or a gig to get the gang moving, Austin's got you covered.

FLYING SOLO
Laid-back night
Hosting up to three music acts each night, The Saxon Pub is sure to tickle your eardrums, whatever your jam. If you're by yourself, post up at the bar and enjoy a show (or two).

IN A PAIR
Jazz for two
Take your date to The Elephant Room for some swinging jazz. As well as great tunes, this underground joint serves up tasty cocktails and a huge roster of beer.

FOR A CROWD
Tunes for the crew
With a history spanning over 150 years, The Historic Scoot Inn is, well, historic. This place specializes in eclectic indie bands. Bring some like-minded friends, grab a drink, and find a good spot to listen to whoever's playing the outdoor stage.

THE CONTINENTAL CLUB

Map 5; 1315 South Congress Avenue, South Congress; ///splat.salt.drill;
www.continentalclub.com

The Continental Club has lived many lives since it first opened in
1955. First, it was an upmarket supper club, then a burlesque and
blue-collar bar, before turning into its present incarnation: Austin's
premier venue for roots rock, country, and rockabilly. Junior Brown,
Link Wray, Robert Plant – you name them, they've played here.

» Don't leave without checking out the Continental Gallery upstairs.
This intimate speakeasy-style bar is great for dates.

THE FAR OUT LOUNGE

Map 6; 8504 South Congress Avenue, South Congress;
///spicy.cobras.curated; www.thefaroutaustin.com

Follow the young crowd to this South Congress spot for some good ol'
rock 'n' roll. (Fun fact: UT student Janis Joplin played here long before
Woodstock.) Things get pretty lively by the mural-backed outdoor
stage, while more intimate gigs take place in the old stone cottage.

MOHAWK

Map 1; 912 Red River Street, Red River Cultural District;
///begins.having.mule; www.mohawkaustin.com

With a name like that, it'll probably come as no surprise that
Mohawk reps Austin's alt-rock and indie scene. It's super-busy
and more than a little rowdy, so make like the cool kids and get
here early. (The middle terrace has the best views.)

Culture Live

Austin may be the Live Music Capital of the World, but it could also claim the title of live culture capital, too. The city is home to some excellent – and inclusive – poetry slams and comedy clubs.

AUSTIN POETRY SLAM

Map 2; 1911 Aldrich Street Suite 120B, Mueller;
///recent.inserted.random; www.barrelofunatx.com

Every Tuesday night, Barrel O' Fun at the Alamo Drafthouse hosts one of the oldest and most competitive poetry slams in Texas. Accompanied by raucous yells of approval, a dozen contestants deliver powerful performances on big topics such as religion in the Deep South, "anti-social networks," and toxic masculinity, before being scored on their performance.

THE VELVEETA ROOM

Map 1; 521 East 6th Street, Red River Cultural District;
///trucked.pans.briefer; www.thevelveetaroom.com

The best comedy spots are teeny tiny. Take The Velveeta Room, a small venue on the corner of Dirty Sixth, where comics perform to a pretty sparse audience. Sound like a tough crowd? The performers know that if they can win over this room, they can make any audience laugh. It's a great place to see an intimate show from the occasional superstar, or superstar-in-waiting. Kerry Awn, Maggie Maye, Matt Sadler, and Howard Beecher, to name a few, have all performed here.

>> Don't leave without signing up for a spot on next Thursday's open mic night. The audience will decide whether you're a comic genius or if you should stick to your day job.

FALLOUT THEATER
Map 1; 616 Lavaca Street, Civic District; ///pipes.braved.enable; www.falloutcomedy.com

Part comedy club, part training center, Fallout Theater is committed to fostering new stand-up, sketch, and improv talent. The eight-week-long comedy classes require commitment, but anyone can get involved in the immersive and interactive shows. Friday night's "F*** This Week" is particularly popular; audience members compete to decide who has had the worst seven days and then the cast makes up a show based around the winning life fail. Cathartic or what?

Try it!
TEST YOUR JOKES

Every other Wednesday at 7pm, Fallout Theater runs a free improv class. It's all very low pressure, so, even if you don't have the X factor, you're guaranteed a good time and plenty of laughs.

COLDTOWNE THEATER

Map 4; 4803 Airport Boulevard Unit C, Hyde Park; ///noted.purest.lush;
www.coldtownetheater.com

It may sound like a cliché, but it really does help to laugh in the face of adversity. And that's exactly what ColdTowne's founders did. The club was created in 2005 by comedians who evacuated from New Orleans in the wake of Hurricane Katrina. They had to live together and beg for food here in Austin, but the result was a tight-knit improv troupe that became so popular it opened its own theater and training center. Today, C-Towne is dedicated to alternative comedy, with improv and sketch classes, and live shows seven nights a week.

THE HIDEOUT THEATRE

Map 1; 617 Congress Avenue, Downtown; ///former.radar.speaking;
www.hideouttheatre.com

From the street, Hideout might look like any old coffee shop, but as you move farther away from the counter, the sound of whirring espresso machines is replaced with peels of laughter. Hideout's two theaters host stand-up comedy, performance art, and musical sketches, but it's the improv that's earned it a dedicated local following. It's quite surprising really, given how personal these shows can get, with performers asking the audience for embarrassing material (like awkward encounters with mothers-in-law) to seamlessly insert into their hilarious monologues. Those on first dates might want to arrive early to nab a seat at the back.

» Don't leave without ordering a Gorilla Mocha from the coffee shop out front to slurp while you watch the show.

SPOKEN AND HEARD

Map 4; 5775 Airport Boulevard Suite 725, Highland;
///coins.slipped.stormy; www.kickbuttcoffee.com

It requires bravery to take the mic, but everyone's guaranteed a confidence boost at Spoken and Heard. It doesn't matter if the verse-slinger is a novice or established, whether they're reading from their phone, a scrap of paper, or are accompanied by a guitar, the inclusive crowd cheers one and all at this Sunday open mic night. Still got stage fright? Kick Butt Coffee (which hosts Spoken and Heard) serves up $4 Bloody Marys and mimosas, as well as java, all night.

» Don't leave without asking about the next Kick Butt kung fu class. **The café's owner, and martial arts grandmaster, Thomas Gohring will teach you some moves.**

ESTHER'S FOLLIES

Map 1; 525 East 6th Street, Downtown; ///beefed.prosper.ledge;
www.esthersfollies.com

In 1977, Michael Shelton and Shannon Sedwick threw an April Fool's party in a leased bar on seedy 6th Street, and local singers, poets, musicians, and comics all rocked up to perform. They ended the night with a dance around a lawn sprinkler in a campy homage to aquatic-choreographer Esther Williams, and Esther's Follies was born. The high-adrenaline party atmosphere remains, but this talent-show-comedy-club hybrid isn't called Texas's answer to *SNL* for nothing. The comic sketches, musical performances, and magic tricks skewer political parties, cultural phenomena, and local happenings with razor-sharp wit.

LGBTQ+ Scene

Austin is often called "a blue dot in a sea of red." This city is endlessly LGBTQ+ friendly, with an ever-changing host of new queer venues, drag shows, and nightclubs alongside some time-tested favorites.

HIGHLAND LOUNGE

Map 1; 404 Colorado Street, Warehouse District;
///lemmings.present.issued; www.highlandlounge.com

Guy Town (the area now known as the Warehouse District) was brimming with brothels, saloons, and beer halls till 20th-century anti-sex work laws turned this entertainment district into an industrial area. Fast-forward to the 1980s and many of the warehouses were abandoned – but not for long. Austin's jubilant LGBTQ+ scene claimed the area, setting up inclusive clubs like the Highland Lounge.

RAIN ON 4TH

Map 1; 217 West 4th Street, Warehouse District;
///voice.teamed.firmer; www.rainon4th.com

This joint is pumping on weekends, with punters squeezing in for a spot to live their best lives. The packed crowd – which leans fella heavy, though not exclusively – is always just-got-paid happy and

Swing by on Thursday for fun and guilt-free bingo – proceeds benefit a HIV and AIDS charity.

up for dancing all night long. And with the DJ blasting crowd favorites (hello, Gaga), who can blame them for taking to the glowing dance floor?

OILCAN HARRY'S

Map 1; 211 West 4th Street, Warehouse District; ///cult.surreal.solve; www.oilcanharrys.com

It may lack the polish that characterizes its sleeker Warehouse neighbors, but that's part of Oilcan Harry's charm. The beer is cheap, everyone seems to know everyone else, and there's a side gay sports bar, called Score, where jocks go to play darts and pool, and watch the game. If you're looking for glitz, though, Harry's got you. Catch your favorite queens from *RuPaul's Drag Race* on Sunday nights during Showtime. Sashay this way.

CHEER UP CHARLIES

Map 1; 900 Red River Street, Red River Cultural District; ///coached.premises.painters; www.cheerupcharlies.com

With kombucha on tap, a vegan food truck out front, and painfully cool bands playing its two stages, Cheer Up Charlies is the hipster player on Austin's LGBTQ+ scene. Co-owners and power couple Tamara Hoover and Maggie Lea's first love was music, but there are plenty of other events, like queer storytelling, sex ed, and drag shows.

» Don't leave without trying one of the kombucha cocktails. We love the Golden Ticket, made with kombucha, whiskey, and ginger.

Liked by the locals

"Most cities have a very specific area of town that is 'LGBTQ+.' All of Austin is welcoming and we don't have a specific 'gayborhood.' Be it housing, shopping, brunch, nightlife, Austin welcomes all, everywhere."

TINA CANNON, PRESIDENT AND CEO OF
AUSTIN LGBT CHAMBER OF COMMERCE

THE IRON BEAR

**Map 1; 301 West 6th Street, Downtown; ///blaring.feared.offices;
www.theironbear.com**

A self-assigned neighborhood bar, The Iron Bear is about the simple things: dirt-cheap beer, solid soul food, and catch-ups with friends. They describe themselves as "a bar for Bears by Bears," but people of all stripes are welcomed here with open arms.

» Don't leave without enjoying a judgment-free dance. The resident DJ's always spinning classic tunes.

BUTTERFLY BAR AT THE VORTEX

**Map 3; 2307 Manor Road, Chestnut; ///having.wiggly.scuba;
www.butterflybaraustin.com**

Every second Sunday, Trans and Genderqueer Social (TGQ) takes over this bar-meets-butterfly sanctuary for its monthly meetups. Here, gender-diverse folks can meet allies, get advice, and have a good time. Newcomers are invited to rock up 30 minutes early so that they can be eased into the party – wallflowers rejoice.

VIOLET CROWN SOCIAL CLUB

**Map 2; 1111 East 6th Street, East Cesar Chavez; ///artist.tailors.sagging;
www.violetcrownsocialclub.com**

Frustrated at Austin's lack of lesbian bars, queer collective Where the Girls Go decided to stop moaning and do something about it. They set up Guerrilla Queer Bar, a roving lesbian night that reclaims the city's "straight" bars – seek 'em out at the Violet Crown Social Club.

Game Night

Texans have a competitive streak – football is almost a religion here, after all. And Austinites are no different. Come the evening, they challenge their friends to bowling, mini-golf, sing-offs, and more.

HIGHLAND LANES

Map 6; 8909 Burnet Road, Wooten; ///stars.speakers.trouser; www.highlandlanes.com

With its harsh strip lighting, plain wooden lanes, and no-nonsense vibe, Highland Lanes is an honest-to-goodness bowling alley. There's nothing trendy about it, so don't expect to find DJs or dance floors – just a mixed bunch of locals having a good time. Don some bowling shoes, order a round of White Russians from the *Big Lebowski*-themed bar, and tell your friends to call you "The Dude" if you win.

THE ORIGINAL PINBALLZ ARCADE

Map 6; 8940 Research Boulevard, Wooten; ///bouncing.rinsed.twirls; www.pinballzarcade.com

Where do game-loving Austinites go to celebrate their birthdays? The Original Pinballz Arcade. Over 200 pinball machines in just about every theme you can imagine, from Aerosmith to *The X-Files*, keep

On Wayback Wednesdays, select games are only 25 cents to play, just as they were in the 80s.

celebrating groups flipping and pulling all night long. Add almost 250 other arcade games and a BYO policy, and it's no wonder this place is so popular.

CIDERCADE AUSTIN

Map 5; 600 East Riverside Drive, Riverside; ///flushed.imagined.slogged; www.cidercadeaustin.com

Dallas may be the home of the Bishop Cider Co., which gave sugary apple juice a vegan-friendly makeover, but Austin has adopted its Cidercade as its own. This unique concept unites cider and arcade games in a sweet deal – the $10 entry grants unlimited game play and access to the tap wall, which drips with hard cider, seltzer, and kombucha.

>> Don't leave without buying a cup and taking advantage of the unlimited refills from the Maine Root soda fountain.

THE GOLDEN GOOSE

Map 5; 2034 South Lamar Boulevard, South Lamar; ///cookery.trample.performs; www.thegooseaustin.com

Okay, this one is more about embracing your inner retiree than inner kid. The Golden Goose takes shuffleboard very seriously; it has an intimidating 22 ft (7 m) table. But don't worry if you're a beginner, you'll still have an awesome time. Grab the gang (so long as you're in multiples of two), and learn why your granddaddy has long been obsessed with shuffleboard.

PLAYLAND SKATE CENTER
Map 6; 8822 McCann Drive, North Shoal Creek;
///opens.detection.tycoons; www.playlandskatecenter.net

When this skating rink opened in 1973, it became a firm date night staple, with flares-clad couples roller skating under the disco balls. These days, Playland Skate Center is mostly circled by kids – except for every Tuesday night, when adults take to the rink. Expect a mix of expert skaters twirling effortlessly under the lazy lights and newbies who rely on the pizza position to slow their roll. Test the mettle of your own crew by seeing which of your friends can stay upright the longest.

PETER PAN MINI-GOLF
Map 5; 1207 Barton Springs Road, Zilker; ///quirky.stumble.kept;
www.peterpanminigolf.com

If the words "mini-golf" conjure up memories of after-school hangouts at strip-mall courses, think again. Peter Pan captures all of the nostalgia and fun of this tiny game but gives it a grown-up spin. They're open pretty late and it's BYO. (Don't worry: they know their tipsy audience well, so the holes aren't that difficult.)

VIGILANTE
Map 6; 7010 Easy Wind Drive, Crestview; ///husbands.drifter.infinite;
www.vigilantebar.com

Clue, Catan, and Battle Sheep – wait, what? As well as the classics, this board game bar has some rogue choices in its extensive catalog. And as a table here comes with unlimited play, you can try out as many games as you like during your time slot. Getting hungry? Push the call button under the table. There's no need to interrupt play, even to get food and drinks. And every game needs snacks.

» Don't leave without booking one of the themed rooms for your next game night with the gang. With its old-world vibe, the Guildhall is an obvious choice for fans of Dungeons & Dragons.

EGO'S

Map 5; 510 South Congress Avenue, South Congress;
///teaspoons.format.prepared; (512) 474-7091

Challenge your friends to a sing-off and see who can hit a pitch-perfect "Galileo." We're pretty sure that this karaoke bar plays other songs too, but "Bohemian Rhapsody" is the top choice. As there are no private rooms here, the crowd always gets involved, providing backing vocals and cheering on the most tone-deaf. So even if you can't hit those high notes, y'all are guaranteed a good time.

Shh!

What screams lumberjack more than axe throwing? Way out in soulless Walnut Creek Business Park, you'll find Class Axe *(www.classaxethrowing. com)*. Here, groups of plaid-shirt-wearing friends face off in an elimination-style tournament. It's hard enough to hit the board itself, let alone a bull's-eye, but that's all part of the fun. And although axes tend to ricochet around the caged lanes, you're in safe hands here.

A night of music in
Downtown

The perfect introduction to the Live Music Capital of the World? A stroll around Downtown after dark. Buskers serenade the streets; the sound of heavy metal, blues, and hip-hop drifts from open windows; and youngsters and old-timers enjoy boot-scootin' fun in honky-tonks. As well as the highest concentration of music venues in the US, this area lures fans with brimming record stores; fun music museums; and quirky, guitar-themed gift shops that stay open well into the evening.

1. Waterloo Records
600 North Lamar
Boulevard, Downtown;
www.waterloorecords.com
///vibe.loosens.town

2. Wild About Music
615 Congress Avenue,
Downtown; www.wild
aboutmusic.com
///feasts.unwell.trace

3. The Cloak Room
1300 Colorado Street,
Downtown; (512) 472-9808
///shocks.upholds.beside

4. Texas Chili Parlor
1409 Lavaca Street,
Downtown; (512) 472-2828
///revived.elbow.minus

5. Antone's
305 East 5th Street,
Downtown; www.
antonesnightclub.com
///abode.outlines.bother

📍 **Driskill Hotel**
///reeling.spoken.talents

📍 **Moody Theater**
///hounded.purist.holds

CLARKSVILLE

ENFIELD ROA

**Hunt for treasure at
WATERLOO
RECORDS**
Looking for an obscure LP?
Chances are you'll find it
here. Sift through the huge
record selection, and, if
you're lucky, catch an
in-store performance.

1

SEAH(

Colora

SOUTH LAMAR BOULEVARD

Butler
Metro Pa

Shoal Creek

Fill up at the
TEXAS CHILI PARLOR

The "chili parlor bar" from Guy Clark's hit song "Dublin Blues" is the ultimate place to try the state dish – chili. Wash it down with a frosty margarita.

Grab a drink at
THE CLOAK ROOM

Choose a tune from the old-school jukebox and then savor a predinner drink at this subterranean dive bar.

4

EAST 15TH STREET

3

WEST 11TH STREET

COLORADO ST

Texas State Capitol

Waller Creek

Rifle through
WILD ABOUT MUSIC

This music-themed store stocks everything from guitars to spoons that look like drum sticks. No, seriously.

*Every Friday and Saturday night, the supposedly haunted **Driskill Hotel** hosts live music performances in its wood-paneled bar.*

EAST 11TH ST

WEST 6TH STREET

2

CONGRESS AVENUE

WEST 5TH STREET

WEST 4TH STREET

GUADALUPE STREET

STREET

STREET

SAN JACINTO BLVD

5

Follow your ear to
ANTONE'S

Groove to good ol' fashioned rock 'n' roll at the club that's played host to legends like B.B. King, Buddy Guy, Eric Clapton, and Stevie Ray Vaughan.

DOWNTOWN

I-35

ver

*The **Moody Theater** is the home of TV show Austin City Limits, which has been broadcasting live music performances since 1974.*

EAST CESAR CHAVEZ STREET

| 0 meters | 400 |
| 0 yards | 400 |

OUTDOORS

When the mercury soars, Austinites seek relief in the great outdoors. Frisbees are flung in the city's parks, and bathing suits are donned at cooling swimming holes.

Hiking and Biking

*When you live in the middle of Texas Hill Country,
it's hard to resist getting stuck into nature. So lace up
your boots or pack those panniers, and join the locals
as they set out on one of these trails.*

SOUTHERN WALNUT CREEK TRAIL

**Map 3; start at 5200 Bolm Road, Springdale; ///seated.scarred.loaders;
www.austintexas.gov/department/southern-walnut-creek-trail**

Cycling-obsessed Austinites can't get enough of this 7.5-mile
(12-km) hike-and-bike trail. On weekends, they race along this
asphalt ribbon, winding over rivers and through shaded
undergrowth. (Watch out: shy deer often dart across the path.) It's
relatively flat until the last mile, when it quickly becomes evident
why it's called Texas Hill Country.

HILL OF LIFE TRAIL

**Map 6; start at 1710 Camp Craft Road, Barton Creek;
///outbid.roofed.hounded**

If plummeting 1,500 ft (450 m) in just three minutes sounds like your
kind of thing, then grab your mountain bike and take on the Hill of
Life. The trail starts at the top of the hill, before hurtling down the

rocky, stepped descent to Barton Creek, taking in wide-sweeping views of the Greenbelt along the way. Don't have a bike? Don't sweat it – you can tackle the trail on foot, but, unless you're tuck-duck-and-rolling, it'll probably take longer than three minutes.

» Don't leave without taking a dip at the Hill of Life Dam before looping back to the trail head. You'll appreciate the chance to cool off before climbing back up the hill.

WALLER CREEK GREENBELT TRAIL
Map 2; start at 703 East 6th Street, Downtown; ///icons.dragons.minerals
When the kids get antsy and need entertaining, parents make for this flat, family-friendly trail. Here, youngsters can let off steam while learning, as they gather around their mom and dad's smartphones to listen to UT's Waller Creek Walking Tour. This free app points out sights, plants, and animals along the route.

Shh!

If you're craving an escape from the crowds on South First and SoCo Avenue, make a break for Blunn Creek Greenbelt. Located just a couple of blocks to the east in Travis Heights, this 40-acre (16-ha), creek-side park has shaded trails, hilly overlooks, and rugged nature. Although it's more of a stroll than a hike, the 1.5-mile (1-km) Blunn Creek loop, which skirts the creek, is a pretty and quiet path that will transport you far away from the feverish city streets.

SHOAL CREEK TRAIL

**Map 4; start at 3108 North Lamar Boulevard, Bryker Woods;
///trick.describe.mondays**

In the precious hours before the mercury soars, the whole of Austin seems to hit the city's oldest trail, which traces Shoal Creek from Bryker Woods into the heart of Downtown. Join the hordes of cyclists, dog walkers, strollers, and runners on their morning ritual. Sound overcrowded? Don't worry – southern politeness means that you'll easily navigate even the narrowest part of the trail. And, boy, does it get narrow when it skirts between jutting cliff faces and steep, heart-in-mouth slopes.

COVERT PARK

**Map 6; 3800 Mount Bonnell Road, Mount Bonnell;
///hiding.zooms.diamond**

When they're in need of a thigh-burning adventure, locals lace up their sneakers or mount their bikes, and head to Covert Park. Sure, it's a pretty steep climb to the summit of Mount Bonnell, but

Try it!
LEARN TO CLIMB

For a different perspective on Barton Creek, take a climbing class with Rock-About (www.rock-about.com). You'll learn how to scale natural rock walls safely, while enjoying great views of the creek below.

the view at the top's well worth the burning calves. From here, you can see the skyline in its entirety, along with the dramatic vistas of the Colorado River aka Town Lake (and, not to mention, the dreamy lakefront mansions). If you don't want to be surrounded by crowds of selfie-snapping out-of-towners and flirting teens, plan your hike or ride for the early morning.

ANN AND ROY BUTLER HIKE-AND-BIKE TRAIL

Map 5; start at Lamar Bridge, Downtown; ///star.competent.magical; www.austintexas.gov

The Ann and Roy Butler Hike-and-Bike Trail has a story that sounds like something out of US sitcom *Parks and Recreation*. In 1971, Ann Butler (wife of mayor Roy Butler) met up with her friend (and First Lady) Lady Bird Johnson in London, England. Sat on a patio overlooking the Thames Path, they were struck with the idea of creating a river trail in their hometown. The women started fundraising immediately, with Ann roping in local garden clubs to maintain the plants. The result was coined the Ann and Roy Butler Hike-and-Bike Trail. But that's a mouthful, so most locals just call this 10-mile (16-km) path the Town Lake Trail. Now surrounded by skyscrapers and punctuated with modern sculptures, the path's landscape may have changed, but it's still the community space that Ann and Lady Bird envisaged.

» **Don't leave without** caffeinating up at The Perch on the northern shore of the lake. This coffee shop has a perennially sun-drenched patio that'll be hard to leave when it's time to continue on the trail.

Alfresco Fitness

All those tacos and BBQ feasts can take their toll. The good news? Austin has no shortage of outdoor fitness classes and workouts, where you can work up a sweat while also enjoying the city.

STAND-UP PADDLEBOARDING

Map 2; Lady Bird Lake, East Cesar Chavez; ///roses.moods.flatten; www.austintexas.gov/page/lady-bird-lake

On scorching weekends, half of the city seems to bring their stand-up paddleboards to Lady Bird Lake (the other half are at a swimming hole, naturally). And with a cooling breeze, killer views, and a gentle core workout, who can blame them? Grab a SUP from one of the many rentals that line the shore, and join the locals on the water.

OUTDOOR YOGA

Map 6; 8504 South Congress Avenue, South Congress; ///maps.slice.alleges; www.blackswanyoga.com

The city that gave the world superstar online teacher Adriene Mishler sure isn't lacking in yoga studios. And Austin has plenty of outdoor classes to choose from, where yogis can salute the sun rather than studio lights. Take Black Swan Yoga's "Yoga in the Yard" at The Far

Out Lounge. With all proceeds being donated to a rotating group of local nonprofits, this Sunday morning flow is sure to give that all-important, feel-good glow.

AUSTIN RUNNERS CLUB

Map 5; 1300 South Congress Avenue, South Congress;
///interval.promotes.tested; www.austinrunners.org

We get it: running can be intimidating. Not so at the Austin Runners Club. Since 1974, this nonprofit has been making the sport more inclusive by setting up running groups for everyone: relaxed runs, classes for distance runners, and a body-positive women's group. There are loads of groups and routes, but our fave is the Tuesday morning run from Jo's Coffee to the Texas Capitol.

» Don't leave without joining your running mates for a post-run coffee or happy hour. No judgment if you don't order a mocktail.

THURSDAY NIGHT SOCIAL RIDE

Map 2; Nash Hernandez Senior Road 1100, East Cesar Chavez;
///pillow.sunshine.floating; www.socialcyclingaustin.org

Social Cycling Austin's founders Keith Byrd and John Acker set out to get more "butts on bikes." And, from the look of the 250-strong crowd of cyclists that meet for the Thursday Night Social Ride, we reckon they succeeded. Why is it so popular? The winning formula of sweat, socializing, and sweet drinks. The 10-mile (16-km) route changes each week, but the structure is always the same: meet over brews at Festival Beach, ride to a park for more drinks, then end up at a bar.

BALLET AUSTIN

Map 1; 501 West 3rd Street, Downtown; ///aviation.exactly.cloud;
www.balletaustin.org

On top of a parking garage, groups of friends clad in their fave
workout outfits learn how to plié with Austin's professional ballet
company. Choose between Dance the Deck (hip-hop cardio) and
Rooftop Workouts (barre) and come prepared to sweat.

» **Don't leave without** popping across the street to the Butler Center
for Dance & Fitness to see the pros in action.

TAIJI & QIGONG MEDITATION CENTER

Map 4; west side of Shoal Creek, between 32nd and 34th Streets,
Shoal Creek; ///soaks.along.soothing; www.taichiimmortal.com

Nothing focuses your mind ahead of your start-up's stock market
launch like a tai chi or meditation class. At least that's what Austin's
Silicon Hills office workers think. You'll find them getting into the
zone at Shoal Creek on Tuesday and Thursday mornings, before
heading into the office.

ESQUINA TANGO

Map 2; 209 Pedernales Street, Govalle; ///custom.pouting.spiking;
www.esquinatango.org

Everyone's invited to this nonprofit's donation-based Latin dance
fiesta. Meeting in front of a colorful old church-turned-cultural-center,
a motley assortment of old-timers, moms, and students of all shapes
and sizes dance it up to the sounds of tango, salsa, hip-hop, and jazz.

Liked by the locals

"We offer a unique way to be active in Austin. Our dance and fitness classes aren't just your everyday workouts; they're heaps of fun, too."

VICKI PARSONS, DIRECTOR OF BALLET AUSTIN AND THE
BUTLER CENTER FOR DANCE & FITNESS

Green Spaces

In a city with so many neighborhood parks, it would be a crime to stay indoors. From untamed wildflower preserves to wide open plains, there's something for every nature lover to enjoy.

MCKINNEY FALLS STATE PARK

Map 6; enter at 5808 McKinney Falls Parkway, Dove Springs;
///inkjet.with.showcase

It may just be a short drive from Downtown Austin, but this swath of nature feels like a world away from the city. During the week, it's a quiet affair, with retirees leisurely fishing in the creeks and the odd local indulging in an amble. But when the weekend hits, it's a totally different story. Outdoorsy families descend in droves, their cars packed with camping equipment and picnic supplies, while groups of friends don their sportswear and take to the scenic hiking trails.

MUELLER LAKE PARK

Map 3; enter at 4550 Mueller Boulevard, Mueller; ///bridges.lions.eternity

Looking for a park to suit the whole crew (dogs included)? Austinites will probably recommend this watery oasis. Home to a huge lake, an interactive playscape, and an open-air amphitheater, this epic space

Time your visit with the Texas Farmers' Market *(p101)*, which promises fresh produce and gourmet treats.

will keep little ones and pups busy for hours. As for the adults, art installations have popped up all over the park, plus there are several great cafés around the corner.

ZILKER PARK

Map 5; enter at 2207 Lou Neff Road, Zilker; ///groups.snores.nagging

As the sun rises, yogis clutching their freshly made smoothies saunter into this central park for an outdoor session. Throughout the day, workers stop by for a much-needed breath of fresh air, lingering in the botanical garden for a moment of calm. And when school's out, the basketball courts buzz, and breezy Barton Springs pool *(p182)* fills up with families cooling down. Zilker's also home to the uber-cool Austin City Limits music festival. In a nutshell, this park has it all.

>> **Don't leave without** attending a free musical at Zilker Hillside Theater, the park's outdoor stage.

BARTON CREEK GREENBELT

Map 6; enter at 3755 South Capital of Texas Highway, Barton Hills; ///join.exhale.advising; www.austinparks.org/barton-creek-greenbelt

Ask any local where they go on their downtime and they'll likely say "the Greenbelt." And although there are many greenbelts in this city, they'll be talking about this 7-mile (11-km) stretch. So what's all the fuss about? Barton Creek is a haven for outdoor enthusiasts, with multiple hiking trails, plus climbing and swimming spots. And trust us when we say that you'll be grateful for the last if you take to the trails in the summer.

Solo, Pair, Crowd

This is a city surrounded by nature, with endless possibilities for an outdoor adventure.

FLYING SOLO

Art park for one

In need of a bit of R&R? Take a meditative stroll through the Umlauf Sculpture Garden. The woody realms here are dotted with striking bronze figurine sculptures by American sculptor Charles Umlauf.

IN A PAIR

Lakeside stroll for two

For an alternative Downtown catch-up, pack a picnic and walk to the top of Doug Sahm Hill Summit. If you time your hike right, you'll be rewarded with sunset views.

FOR A CROWD

Skinny dipping with the gang

Hang out with your crew at Hippie Hollow, the only clothing-optional park in all of Texas. It's tucked into a corner of Lake Travis, and, when the brutal heat sets in, there's no better place to shed your clothing (or your inhibitions).

MAYFIELD PARK AND NATURE PRESERVE

Map 6; enter at 3505 West 35th Street, Mount Bonnell;
///dart.manuals.widgets; www.mayfieldpreserve.org

This tranquil estate features lush flower gardens, elegant palm trees, and a picturesque cottage. No surprises, then, that it's a favorite for wedding receptions and engagements. If you'd rather swerve the displays of affection by the lily pad ponds, make a beeline for one of the many walking trails that weave around the outskirts. Oh, and watch out for Mayfield's rather ostentatious residents; brilliantly colored peacocks who strut around and show off their plumage to visitors. They're hard to miss.

LADY BIRD JOHNSON WILDFLOWER CENTER

Map 6; enter at 4801 La Crosse Avenue, South Austin;
///teller.luckily.buoyancy; www.wildflower.org

Get up close and personal with more than 970 species of native Texas plants at this ecological haven. Founded in 1982 by the former First Lady and her friend, Helen Hayes, Austin's favorite wildflower center is brimming with vibrant local flora all year round – though the springtime display from March to mid-April is a real showstopper. For those who aren't fussy about flowers, the center also hosts a variety of events, including photography classes, live music nights, and yoga sessions.

» Don't leave without climbing to the top of the Observation Tower for sweeping views of the gardens and surrounding countryside.

Swimming Spots

Central Texas has four seasons: summer, summer, summer, and winter. And with scorching temperatures for much of the year, swimming is a necessity, as well as a fun way to spend the day.

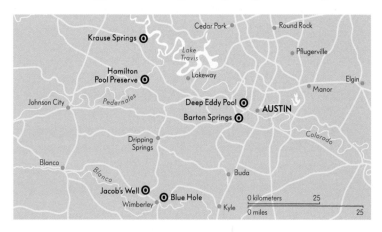

DEEP EDDY POOL

401 Deep Eddy Avenue, Old West Austin; ///beams.horses.sublet;
www.austintexas.gov/department/deep-eddy-pool

Say hello to the oldest artificial swimming pool in Texas. Deep Eddy has had a party vibe since it first opened in 1915. At the time, it was the centerpiece of the Deep Eddy Bathing Beach resort, offering vacationers silent movies, trapeze shows, and Lorena's Diving Horse, which launched itself into the water from a 50-ft (15-m) platform. You'll be pleased to hear that the dodgy animal-related attractions are long gone, but the outdoor screenings remain, albeit with a millennial makeover. Hit up Splash Party Nights between June and August, when locals come here to watch their favorite movies while bobbing around in inner tubes.

JACOB'S WELL

1699 Mount Sharp Road, Wimberley; ///pineapples.calculation.subsist
Now this is one cool pool. The gaping mouth of a spring, Jacob's Well acts as the door to a huge underwater cave. Exploring the 140-ft- (42-m-) deep cavern beyond the opening is definitely not recommended (people have died), but it's safe to jump into the water. Just try not to belly flop – there's usually a GoPro-wielding crowd hanging out here.

HAMILTON POOL PRESERVE

23400 Hamilton Road, Dripping Springs;
///ivories.enforcement.grace; (512) 264-2740
Fed by a waterfall and enclosed by a limestone grotto, this jade-green pool is a cut above your average swimming hole. And it has the exclusive vibe to match, with Austinites making reservations weeks in advance for the chance to hang out here.
» **Don't leave without** hiking in nearby Reimers Ranch Park once you've dried off. Just be prepared to need another dip afterward – the rocky and steep terrain is sure to induce a sweat.

KRAUSE SPRINGS

Mike Wall Lane, Spicewood; ///shrub.rhapsody.regions;
www.krausesprings.net

What was once a popular spot for baptisms has become a haven for beer-swilling sunbathers. So bring a cooler full of tallboys, pack your best swimsuit, and get here early — it's so popular that it has a one in, one out policy.

BARTON SPRINGS

2131 William Barton Drive, Zilker; ///enigma.freedom.surveyed;
www.austintexas.gov/department/barton-springs-pool

A community of thick-skinned regulars swim laps here through the winter, swearing that it's the best way to start the day. Mere mortals wait for the first sign of summer, when this spring-fed pool becomes the coolest place to be in the city. Literally.

» Don't leave without popping into the Nature and Science Center next door to learn about the Barton Springs salamander. This endangered species has become a bit of a hometown hero.

BLUE HOLE

Blue Hole Lane, Wimberley; ///circuitry.oracle.migrations;
www.cityofwimberley.com

Framed by arched trees and a manicured lawn, this impossibly blue pool looks like something straight out of a Disney movie. Do as the locals do by dropping into the water from a rope swing and floating along in an inner tube.

Liked by the locals

"My swim at Barton Springs is my religion and the pool my church. There is a peace there. When you first jump in, it's cold – I always dread it – but, once you get used to it, you feel like you're swimming in the best pool in the universe."

CHRISTIANO PRADO, OWNER OF BRAZILIAN CHEESE BREAD BRAND TAPIO FOODS AND ARDENT SWIMMER

Nearby Getaways

Sure, the locals love their city, but sometimes a change of scene is just the ticket. Luckily, Austin is surrounded by friendly towns and wild state parks, perfect for those itching to hit the open road.

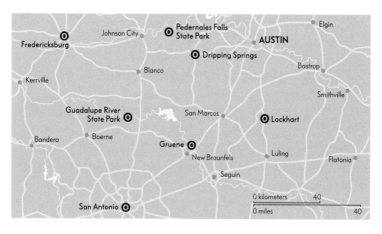

DRIPPING SPRINGS

30-minute drive from Austin; www.destinationdrippingsprings.com

The perfect remedy after a long week of work? Sipping local beer and spirits in the Hill Country, an area just outside Austin that's brimming with breweries and distilleries. And the perfect place to base yourself? Dripping Springs. Full disclaimer: the town's not much to write home about, but the drinking dens located nearby (Deep Eddy Vodka Distillery, Twisted X Brewery, and Treaty Oak Distilling) are top-notch.

GUADALUPE RIVER STATE PARK

1.5-hour drive from Austin;

www.tpwd.texas.gov/state-parks/guadalupe-river

If you don't fancy spending your dollar on distillery tours, here's a more affordable option: tubing down the scenic Guadalupe River with a pack of sodas. It's always a good-time vibe at this state park, with raucous young locals plunging into the fresh water and floating downstream with their inflatable coolers carrying their drinks. It's cheap, cheerful, and a whole lot of fun on a holiday weekend.

LOCKHART

1-hour bus from CARTS at Plaza Saltillo Station, Austin;

www.lockhart-tx.org

If you think Austin is BBQ-obsessed, think again. Lockhart is *all* about BBQ food. There's a smokehouse on nearly every corner of this quaint town (Black's Barbecue is our favorite), and locals even host an annual event dedicated to the food: the Western Swing and Barbecue Festival. Add super-friendly residents, who'll happily debate who serves up the best BBQ grub with day-tripping Austinites, and you've got yourself the tastiest getaway in Texas.

» Don't leave without checking out Caldwell County Courthouse. It's quite the looker and was featured in the 90s classic *What's Eating Gilbert Grape.*

PEDERNALES FALLS STATE PARK

1-hour drive from Austin; www.tpwd.texas.gov/state-parks/pedernales-falls

When Friday finally comes, Austin's office workers pack up the car and drive out to this favorite state park. They'll likely give the eponymous waterfall (and camera-wielding visitors that come with it) a wide berth, and head for the trails instead. These quiet, wooded paths are exactly what the doctor ordered: meandering for miles without seeing a soul is genuinely rather good for the soul. After a day's hike, it's a cool swim in the creeks and a night under the stars. And, breathe.

GRUENE

50-minute drive from Austin; www.gruenetexas.com

For a real slice of the Lone Star State, head to this off-the-radar town. Gruene (pronounced "Green") looks just like it did when German immigrants established the place way back in the 1840s, so there's history to boot plus some pretty photogenic storefronts. Take a wander around the town and don't miss the quirky shops; with names like Pookie Jane's Boutique and Gruene with Envy, how could you resist?

» Don't leave without trying some two-step at Gruene hall, the oldest continually running dance hall in Texas.

SAN ANTONIO

1.5-hour drive from Austin; www.visitsanantonio.com

When Austin starts to feel a little small, culture-craving 20-somethings hop on the train to San Antonio. It's the next big city south of the capital, and it's packed with things to do. On the bucket list? The iconic Alamo monument to Texas independence, the Japanese Tea Gardens, and the gorgeous River Walk. But that's not all. This city is also home to the Texas grocery institution H-E-B – okay, we know it doesn't sound super exciting, but shelves lined with Texan brands really get the locals hyped. Young guns also love the long roster of festivals San Antonio hosts; head over when the Fiesta Primavera or Dia de Los Muertos events are on and you'll see the very best of this lively city.

FREDERICKSBURG

1.5-hour drive from Austin; www.visitfredericksburgtx.com

Not to go on about the booze in the Hill Country, but we've got one more recommendation for y'all: wine-lover's haven Fredericksburg. This day trip destination is the epicenter of the Texas wine movement and a favorite among groups dressed in their summer best and couples partial to a glass of the good stuff. And with 50 local vineyards here, plus some of the Hill Country's best fine-dining options, it's easy to see why.

Try it!
FORAGE FOR FOOD

Texas Hill Country isn't just about wine. Foraging Texas (www.foragingtexas.com) runs classes all across this beautiful area, helping you become an expert in seeking out edible and medicinal plants.

A day out in
idyllic Zilker

Austin is an oasis in an arid state, and locals take advantage of the great outdoors at every opportunity. And nowhere is this more evident than in the wonderfully green, waterfront neighborhood of Zilker. Come the weekend, Austinites flock here to work up a sweat, take a dip in the water, and soak up the city views while chilling out in a park or on a patio.

1. Umlauf Sculpture Garden
605 Azie Morton Road, Zilker; www.umlauf sculpture.org/yoga
///youth.emblem.drifting

2. Ann and Roy Butler Hike-and-Bike Trail
Zilker
///pouting.wisely.nation

3. Casa de Luz
1701 Toomey Road, Zilker
www.casadeluz.org
///alive.hops.embedded

4. Butler Metro Park
1000 Barton Springs Road, Zilker; www.austinparks.org/ butler-park
///deposits.scooter.horns

5. Peter Pan Mini-Golf
1207 Barton Springs Road, Zilker; www.peterpan minigolf.com
///quirky.stumble.kept

6. ATX Food Co.
517 South Lamar Boulevard, Zilker; www.atxfoodco.com
///enabling.rescue.rankings

Auditorium Shores Dog Park
///supply.arrives.headache

Colorado River

Zilker Park

Barton Creek

1

Stretch it out at the UMLAUF SCULPTURE GARDEN
Salute the sun (and several sculptures) at an all-level morning yoga class in the sculpture garden. It's an idyllic way to kick off the day.

AVENUE

KINNEY

West Cesar Chavez Street

West Cesar Chavez Street

North Lamar Boulevard

0 meters 400
0 yards 400

DOWNTOWN

Walk along the ANN AND ROY BUTLER HIKE-AND-BIKE TRAIL

Tracing the shore of the Colorado River, aka Town Lake, this trail grants unrivaled views of the city skyline. Choose a 3-mile or 5-mile loop depending on how energetic you feel.

2

Austinites are famously dog-obsessed and, with a skyscraper backdrop, Auditorium Shores Dog Park is the city's most scenic off-leash spot.

West Riverside Drive

3

Tuck in at CASA DE LUZ

Ravenous after all that exercise? We've got you. Take a seat on the plant-filled patio and savor some tasty vegan grub.

4

Check out the view from the BUTLER METRO PARK

Trek up to the top of the observation hill and take in the view of Austin's skyline reflected in the lazy waters of Town Lake.

East Bouldin Creek

ZILKER

Barton Springs Road

5

Tee off at PETER PAN MINI-GOLF

You don't need to be a pro to enjoy a putt around. Gulp in fresh air as you swing your way around one of Peter Pan's fun-filled courses.

6

Savor plant-based fare at ATX FOOD CO.

Cardiologist Dr. Joel Kahn serves up 100 percent plant-based dishes from his bright green truck. Tuck into some vegan tacos and then grab some sea moss to go.

South Lamar Boulevard

South 5th Street

South 1st Street

BOULDIN CREEK

With a little research and preparation, this city will feel like a home away from home. Check out these websites to ensure a healthy, safe stay in Austin.

Austin
DIRECTORY

SAFE SPACES

Austin is known for being bighearted, but should you feel uneasy at any point or want to find your community, there are spaces catering to different sexualities, demographics, and religions.

www.austintexas.org/plan-a-trip/cultural-heritage

The city's very useful official tourism guide has links to resources for nonwhite groups.

www.linktr.ee/womenofcolorcollectiveatx

Providing safe spaces and a community for women of color.

www.outyouth.org

Serves young members of Central Texas's LGBTQ+ community, with support groups, counseling services, and events.

www.pflagaustin.org

Runs free support groups for members of the LGBTQ+ community and their allies.

www.shalomaustin.org

An inclusive Jewish-based cultural and community center.

HEALTH

Health care in the US isn't free, so it's important to take out comprehensive health insurance for your visit. If you do need medical assistance, there are many pharmacies and hospitals across the city.

www.austintexas.gov/department/health

Lists local public health services.

www.kindclinic.org

A sexual health and wellness clinic offering free services.

www.rxlist.com/pharmacy/
austin-tx_pharmacies.htm
*A comprehensive list of pharmacies
and hospitals in the Austin area.*

www.stdavids.com
*Resource detailing hospitals and their
services throughout Austin.*

www.waterloocounseling.org
*A nonprofit that provides affordable
mental health counseling and therapy
to all, with support groups for members
of the LGBTQ+ community.*

TRAVEL SAFETY ADVICE
Before you travel – and while you're
here – always keep tabs on the latest
regulations in Austin and the US.

**www.austintexas.org/plan-a-trip/
visitor-health-safety**
*The city's official information site, with
further details on visitor health and
safety available.*

www.cdc.gov
*National public health institute offering
disease prevention and guidance.*

www.texasready.gov
*Weather forecasts and advisories,
including flood and hurricane alerts.*

www.travel.state.gov
*Latest travel safety information from the
US government.*

ACCESSIBILITY
Austin is often hailed as being one of
the most accessible cities in the US, and
most venues and services are accessible
to all people. These resources will help
make your trips go smoothly.

**www.austintexas.gov/department/
travelers-disabilities-and-medical-
conditions-airport**
*Services and information for navigating
the airport.*

**www.austintexas.org/austin-insider-
blog/post/sensory-accessibility-
austin**
*A list of accessible venues on the city's
official tourism site.*

www.capmetro.org/accessibility
*Information on using Austin's buses and
trains, including free travel training
sessions for wheelchair users.*

**www.traviscountytx.gov/health-
human-services/deaf-services/
resources**
*Resources to assist Austin's Deaf and
Hard of Hearing community.*

INDEX

ACKNOWLEDGMENTS

Meet the illustrator

Award-winning British illustrator David Doran is based in a studio by the sea in Falmouth, Cornwall. When not drawing and designing, David tries to make the most of the beautiful area in which he's based; sea-swimming all year round, running the coastal paths and generally spending as much time outside as possible.

With thanks

DK Eyewitness would like to thank the following people for their contribution to the first edition of this book: Jessica Devenyns, Justine Harrington, Nicolai McCrary, Lucy Richards, Rebecca Flynn, Lucy Sara-Kelly, Tania Gomes, and Casper Morris.

MIX
Paper | Supporting responsible forestry
FSC www.fsc.org **FSC™ C018179**

This book was made with Forest Stewardship Council™ certified paper – one small step in DK's commitment to a sustainable future. Learn more at **www.dk.com/uk/information/sustainability**

A NOTE FROM DK EYEWITNESS

The world is fast-changing and it's keeping us folk at DK Eyewitness on our toes. We've worked hard to ensure that this edition of Austin Like a Local is up-to-date and reflects today's favorite places but we know that standards shift, venues close, and new ones pop up in their place. So, if you notice something has closed, we've got something wrong, or left something out, we want to hear about it. Please drop us a line at travelguides@dk.com

THIS EDITION UPDATED BY
Contributor Nicolai McCrary
Senior Editors Lucy Richards, Zoë Rutland
US Senior Editor Jennette ElNaggar
Project Editor Tijana Todorinović
Project Art Editor Bharti Karakoti
Indexer Helen Peters
Cartography Manager Suresh Kumar
Cartographer Ashif
Jacket Designer Laura O'Brien
Jacket Illustrator David Doran
Senior DTP Designer Tanveer Zaidi
Senior Production Editor Jason Little
Senior Production Controller Samantha Cross
Managing Editor Hollie Teague
Senior Managing Art Editor Priyanka Thakur
Art Director Maxine Pedliham
Publishing Director Georgina Dee

First edition 2022

Published in Great Britain by Dorling Kindersley Limited, DK, One Embassy Gardens, 8 Viaduct Gardens, London SW11 7BW.

The authorised representative in the EEA is Dorling Kindersley Verlag GmbH. Arnulfstr. 124, 80636 Munich, Germany.

Published in the United States by DK Publishing, 1745 Broadway, 20th Floor, New York, NY 10019, USA.

Copyright © 2022, 2024 Dorling Kindersley Limited
A Penguin Random House Company
24 25 26 27 10 9 8 7 6 5 4 3 2 1

The publishers cannot accept responsibility for any consequences arising from the use of this book, for any material on third party websites, and cannot guarantee that any website address in this book will be a suitable source of travel information.

A CIP catalog record for this book is available from the British Library.

A catalog record for this book is available from the Library of Congress.

ISSN: 1542 1554
ISBN: 978 0 2416 8679 9

Printed and bound in China.

www.dk.com